Match of My Life

LEEDS

KNOW THE SCORE BOOKS PUBLICATIONS

CULT HEROES	Author	ISBN
CHELSEA	Leo Moynihan	1-905449-00-3
NEWCASTLE	Dylan Younger	1-905449-03-8
SOUTHAMPTON	Jeremy Wilson	1-905449-01-1
WEST BROM	Simon Wright	1-905449-02-X

MATCH OF MY LIFE	Editor	ISBN
ENGLAND WORLD CUP	Massarella & Moynihan	1-905449-52-6
EUROPEAN CUP FINALS	Ben Lyttleton	1-905449-57-7
FA CUP FINALS (1953-1969)	David Saffer	1-905449-53-4
FULHAM	Michael Heatley	1-905449-51-8
LEEDS	David Saffer	1-905449-54-2
LIVERPOOL	Leo Moynihan	1-905449-50-X
SHEFFIELD UNITED	Nick Johnson	1-905449-62-3
STOKE CITY	Simon Lowe	1-905449-55-0
SUNDERLAND	Rob Mason	1-905449-60-7
SPURS	Allen & Massarella	1-905449-58-5
WOLVES	Simon Lowe	1-905449-56-9

HARRY HARRIS	Author	ISBN
WORLD CUP DIARY	Harry Harris	1-905449-90-9
HOLD THE BACK PAGE	Harry Harris	1-905449-91-7

AUTOBIOGRAPHY	Author	ISBN
TACKLES LIKE A FERRET (England Cover)	Paul Parker	1-905449-47-X
TACKLES LIKE A FERRET (Manchester United Cover)	Paul Parker	1-905449-46-1

FOOTBALL FICTION	Author	ISBN
BURKSEY	Peter Morfoot	1-905449-49-6
The Autobiography of a Football God		

CRICKET	Author	ISBN
MOML: THE ASHES	Pilger & Wightman	1-905449-63-1
SMILE LIKE U MEAN IT	Paul Smith	1-905449-45-3

FORTHCOMING PUBLICATIONS IN 2007

CULT HEROES	Author	ISBN
CELTIC	David Potter	978-1-905449-08-8
DERBY	David McVay	978-1-905449-06-4
MANCHESTER CITY	David Clayton	978-1-905449-05-7
RANGERS	Paul Smith	978-1-905449-07-1

MATCH OF MY LIFE	Editor	ISBN
BOLTON WANDERERS	David Saffer	978-1-905449-64-4
FA CUP FINALS (1970-1989)	David Saffer	978-1-905449-65-1
HULL	Grahame Lloyd	978-1-905449-66-8
MANCHESTER UNITED	Sam Pilger	978-1-905449-59-0

GENERAL FOOTBALL	Autor	ISBN
OUTCASTS	Steve Menary	978-1-905449-31-6
The Lands FIFA Forgot		
PARISH TO PLANET	Dr Eric Midwinter	978-1-905449-30-9
A History of Football		
MY PREMIERSHIP DIARY	Marcus Hahnemann	978-1-905449-33-0
Reading's Season in the Premiership		

PUB BORE: 1001 incredible facts to amaze your mates with	ISBN
MANCHESTER UNITED	978-1-905449-80-4
NEWCASTLE UNITED	978-1-905449-81-1
SUNDERLAND	978-1-905449-82-8

CRICKET	Author	ISBN
THE 2006/7 ASHES IN PICTURES	Andrew Searle	978-1-905449-44-6
GROVEL!	David Tossell	978-1-905449-43-9
The 1976 West IndiesTour of England		
LEAGUE CRICKET YEARBOOK	Andy Searle	978-1-905449-70-5
MY AUTOBIOGRAPHY	Shaun Udal	978-1-905449-42-2

Match of My Life

LEEDS

Editor: David Saffer

Series Editor: Simon Lowe
Know The Score Books Limited

www.knowthescorebooks.com

First published in the United Kingdom
by Know The Score Books Limited, 2006

Know The Score Books Limited
118 Alcester Road
Studley
Warwickshire
B80 7NT
www.knowthescorebooks.com

A CIP catalogue record is available for this book from the British Library
ISBN-10: 1-905449-54-2   ISBN-13: 978-1-905449-54-5

Jacket and book design by Lisa David
Jacket photography by Thomas Skovsende

Printed and bound in Great Britain
By Cromwell Press, Trowbridge, Wiltshire

Photographs in this book are reproduced by kind permission of:
Colorsport, EMPICS, Paul Varley, Leeds United Football Club

Front cover:

Top The 1992 Championship team show off the coveted trophy

Bottom Left Peter Lorimer and Allan Clarke celebrate yet another goal for Revie's Leeds

Bottom Right Skipper Paul Butler leads the way – hopefully back to the Premiership

Rear cover:

Top Left Revie's men rejoice with the 1972 FA Cup

Top Right A ticket for Leeds' only FA Cup victory, the 1972 defeat of Arsenal

Bottom David Wetherall, serial scorer of winning goals against Manchester United

Editor's Acknowledgements

Putting this book together would not have been possible but for the support of a number of people who I must thank.

Firstly, Match of My Life – Leeds has become a reality because of the vision of series editor Simon Lowe. A Stoke City fan, like all true observers of the game, Simon recognises the deeds of great British club sides and is determined to bring them into the public domain.

I have not yet forgiven Stoke for ending Leeds unbeaten 29-match league run in 1973/74, but Simon's enthusiasm, support and patience throughout our regular phone calls and emails over recent months have been very much appreciated.

Of course, this book would not have become a reality without the agreement of 14 players who have adorned the white shirt of Leeds United to contribute their memories about an unforgettable period in their lives. My sincere thanks to all the players for sharing their own perspective on how iconic moments in the club's history came about, first hand with me. It was an absolute pleasure to spend time with each and every one of them.

I am also particularly grateful to Paul Dews for supplying the Foreword. In recent years, Leeds United supporters have read about the clubs 'ups and downs' through Paul's daily reports in the Yorkshire Evening Post. His insight into the club is unmatched. Paul is now Head of Media at Leeds United and there could be no better person to take on this responsible post at Elland Road.

Finally, to my number one home team: Debbie, Daniella, Abigail and Jake. Thanks as always for putting up with the endless hours tapping away on my laptop and for turning a blind eye to my grumpiness when deadlines approach.

David Saffer
September 2006

Contents

Introduction

Having the opportunity to sit down face-to-face with 13 stars of yester-year and the current Leeds United captain to talk about their favourite matches has been the proverbial "dream come true". Taking on Match of My Life – Leeds, I was determined to chart the club's history from the early days of the Gentle Giant, John Charles, when Leeds came within a whisker of defeating the mighty Arsenal in the FA Cup quarter-finals of 1950 to the modern era via all the glories in between.

My wish became a reality through Len Browning, a hero at Elland Road when 'cup fever' hit then Division Two Leeds for the first time. For Len, the highlight was an extra-time victory at Bolton Wanderers, Nat Lofthouse and all, in a fifth round replay after a monumental tussle.

Next up came seven players from the Revie era and I make no apology for utilising half the book with the escapades of the Don's legendary team. Their deeds formed the very fabric of the club and future teams will always face comparison. Unfair, yes, but all great clubs have a history, and these boys created it.

Paul Reaney concentrated on the early years under Don and skipper Bobby Collins. Just missing the double in 1965 after winning the Division Two title was an amazing effort. The FA Cup semi-final replay win over Manchester United was historic as it earned Leeds a first FA Cup trip to Wembley. Paul remembers it like yesterday.

When I got wind that Terry Cooper was in town, 'Speedy' Reaney organised a meeting. For me, TC was essential because I had this feeling he'd choose the 1968 League Cup success. It was the club's first major trophy and Terry struck the winning goal. Thanks Paul and thanks Terry for agreeing to meet me at such short notice. Away from history, on a personal note, I wanted to cover this game because, like many supporters, I recall the date and circumstances when I first became hooked on a club. Billy and co returned to Leeds for a civic reception 24 hours after landing the League Cup. My granddad, Harry Moss, took me to the victory parade. From then on Leeds United was my team.

Moving on to more memories of '68 and Norman 'Bites Yer Legs' Hunter covered, in his own peerless style, Leeds' titanic battle with Hungarian giants Ferencvaros to became the first British team to win the coveted Fairs Cup. A few months on and Leeds claimed the biggest domestic prize of all, the Division One championship. Having Johnny Giles recall a monumental campaign was terrific, especially hearing his recollection of United's steadfast performance at Anfield that clinched the title before the players walked gingerly towards the Kop to be acclaimed as Champions.

Twelve months later Leeds lost out in a chase for the 'treble'. However, the season was notable for two of the greatest ever Elland Road goals and Eddie Gray took me through every swerve of his never-to-be forgotten solo effort against Burnley before revealing that his favourite was the first 'wonder-goal', a 35-yard chip.

Come 1972 and only one man could recount Leeds' FA Cup triumph in the Centenary final, Allan Clarke. Quite simply, 'Sniffer' headed home the most famous goal in the club's history.

In 1975, refereeing decisions denied us the ultimate prize of the European Cup. But on the way to the final, Leeds dismantled Barcelona, who boasted Cruyff and co in their ranks, in an epic semi-final. Peter Lorimer was the hero at the Nou Camp with a trademark goal and 'Hotshot' recalls a magical night in Europe.

Into the 'wilderness' years of the 1980s and there was little to crow about until King Billy presided over an eventful season in 1986/87. Skipper Brendon Ormsby recalls the day he "lost it" after scoring the winner against Queen's Park Rangers in a FA Cup fifth round clash, before his semi-final hell at Hillsborough.

Towards the 90s and Sergeant Wilko was at the helm. Two of Howard Wilkinson's charges cover a sensational period that resulted in two titles. Zico himself, Mel Sterland, recalls the 1989/90 Division Two success, while Chris Fairclough, so dominant in defence, relives the 1991/92 Championship winning campaign when Leeds overcame Alex Ferguson's Manchester United.

Fergie's team lost out in three league games during the mid-90s. Twice, two goals from stopper David Wetherall did the trick. David reveals all. Come the Millennium and David O'Leary's babes took on all comers and succeeded. When I got together with Dominic Matteo, I was all set to hear about the San Siro, only to discover I was wide of the mark. Dominic does look back at Milan, but the triumph over Arsenal in 2003 when Mark Viduka scored a late scorcher to guarantee safety encapsulated the calm before the storm and defined the era for him.

Finally, I wanted to finish on a high after the shenanigans of recent times and where better than the St. Mary's Stadium last season, where Paul Butler was at the centre of arguably the greatest comeback in Leeds United's history. Three goals adrift at Southampton with 19 minutes left, Paul scored in a historic 4-3 win.

So there you have it, 14 players and 14 stories of goals, guts and glory.

I know there are other games etched in the memory banks, after all who could forget Southampton '72, Old Trafford '81, Wembley '92 and Deportivo La Coruna '01, but there is only space for 14 favourites and I hope you will agree the players were spot on with their selections.

David Saffer
September 2006

Foreword

PAUL DEWS

Football seasons come and go, but we all have moments we cherish forever. It might be a special goal or a memorable away trip. It could be the stunning performance of an individual or the collective effort of a team on a night far away from home when the odds are stacked against them. It may even be the white hot atmosphere of a crowd inside a packed stadium, but for one reason or another we all have our memories, we all have those special favourite moments, those special games. That's one of the beauties of being a football fan.

As a Leeds United supporter I look back on the 1989/90 season as the most memorable of my lifetime. Sure, the club has enjoyed greater success, but for sheer passion and adrenaline, that Second Division title winning season represented a very, very special nine months. From the first game to the last, it was energy sapping, and come those promotion celebrations in Bournemouth, you felt you had been a part of it. I felt I had been a part of it. And you can't take that away.

Every Leeds fan will have their own special year or special game. The first league title winning season in 1968/69 will stand out for some, as will the unbeaten run in 1973/74. There was the FA Cup final victory in 1972 and the run to the Champions League semi-final in 2001. All were precious times. But what you rarely hear or read is the thoughts of those involved. Granted, you get sound bites in the media where the players recall such occasions, but within days they are usually consigned to the archives and it's onto the next thing, whatever that may be.

And that is why this latest offering from David Saffer is something special. David has written a number of books on Leeds United and, as a fanatical supporter, he admits his publications are a labour of love. He has documented the history of the club, recorded an in-depth publication about the European nights, and covered the Revie era in minute detail. But this latest offering gives supporters an insight into the complete history of the club – and the magical games and memorable seasons that really matter – through the eyes of the players themselves. The pages are packed with memories and stories from those who were on the inside and actually involved. Starting in 1950 through to the 2005/06 season, this is a trip down memory lane with a hefty dose of reality, and it makes for a truly fascinating account. David has derived enormous pleasure from speaking to a number of players who have all played a part in the shaping the history of the club. They too enjoyed the chance to wax lyrical about Leeds United and their personal memories of the club. Hopefully, you will enjoy it too.

Paul Dews
Head of Media, Leeds United FC
September 2006

Dedication

To Harry Moss – for taking me to the League Cup victory parade in 1968 and passing me the Tetley Tea trade cards on the quiet.

LEN BROWNING
CENTRE-FORWARD 1946–1951

BORN   30th March 1928, Doncaster
SIGNED   August 1946 as apprentice
LEEDS CAREER   105 games, 46 goals
LEFT   Transferred to Sheffield United, November 1951

Len had strength on the ball, was powerful in the air and possessed pace, which made him a difficult opponent to shake off. Blessed with natural ball control and a clinical strike, Len made his Leeds debut at 18 and was a respected striker during a four-year spell after completing his national service. Twice top scorer, Len was a key player in the side that reached the FA Cup quarter-finals for the first time in the club's history in 1950. After leaving Leeds, Len helped Sheffield United win the Division Two championship in 1953, but ended his Football League career the next season after contracting tuberculosis.

Bolton Wanderers 2 v Leeds United 3

FA Cup Fourth Round replay
Wednesday 1st February 1950

Burnden Park
Attendance 29,440

Leeds United reach the FA Cup quarter-final for first time in their history

Teams

Walter Rowley	**Managers**	Major Frank Buckley
Stan Hanson	1	Harry Searson
John Roberts	2	Jimmy Dunn
Tommy Banks	3	Jim Milburn
Malcolm Barrass	4	Jim McCabe
Matt Gillies	5	John Charles
Don Howe	6	Tommy Burden
Harry McShane	7	David Cochrane
Willie Moir	8	Ray Iggledon
Nat Lofthouse	9	Len Browning
Jack Bradley	10	Frank Dudley
Robert Langton	11	Harold Williams

McShane 53, Lofthouse 70 **Scorers** Dudley 2, 95, Browning 48

Referee: E Plinston

"IT'S AMAZING TO think that over 50 years have passed since I played with John Charles, Tommy Burden, Frank Dudley and Harold Williams under the charge of Major Frank Buckley. My years at Leeds United were full of memories, but sadly only a few of us are still here to tell the tale. As Stanley Matthews, Tommy Lawton, Nat Lofthouse and Tom Finney made headlines in the First Division, we battled away in the Second. We had a useful side and created our own headlines during our FA Cup run in 1950 when we so nearly went all the way. We went out to the eventual winners, Arsenal in the quarter-final, but not before we gave them a mighty scare at Highbury. The high for me was our fourth round battle against First Division Bolton Wanderers, which we won after a replay. A win over Second Division rivals Cardiff meant it was the first time Leeds had reached the quarter-finals. The city was buzzing.

My development as a footballer had a touch of good fortune about it. I was born in Doncaster, but my parents were Salvation Army officers. This meant I lived in different places during my childhood. Before settling in Leeds at the age of 13, I grew up in Ireland and Scotland. Although I lived near Celtic's ground in Glasgow, I followed Rangers. In Leeds, initially I was a right-winger for Quarry Brae School, but switched to centre-forward when I played for Leeds Secondary Modern School.

Like many of my friends, I was desperate to be a footballer. I trained at Elland Road during the evenings, hoping to get spotted. Eventually I gained selection for the West Riding County team, but the game clashed with a match that my School was due to play. I asked permission to play in West Riding's match, but the headmaster refused. When I went ahead and played in the West Riding game I was expelled. It was a real blow as I was in my final year at school and hoped to study maths at Leeds University. My parents were very upset and went to the Local Education Authority, but could do nothing about the headmaster's decision. It was crazy, as a head-master in Huddersfield congratulated another player hoping to make a mark in front of the whole school on his selection.

Sometimes, though, it's helpful to be in the right place at the right time and, being off school, I went to watch an England Youth Club trial match at Elland Road. It would prove my lucky day. A West Riding selector saw me in the crowd and went to speak to an England selector. He suggested I play in the second half. The England selector agreed, but I had to borrow a pair of boots. I scored the only goal of the game and must have impressed watching officials because I was chosen to play for England Youth Clubs against Wales at Ninian Park. We won 4-0 and I scored a hat-trick. I also represented England Youth Clubs against the Air Training Corps at Wembley. It was a real thrill to play at Wembley in front of a sizeable crowd and especially as it was my 18th birthday.

Of that England youth team Tommy McNulty made the grade at Manchester United and suddenly a number of teams wanted to sign me. First Division giants Burnley, Blackpool and Wolves were among the big clubs in for me at the time, but because I lived at home with my mum and dad there was only one club for me. I joined Leeds United in August 1946. Three months later, I signed professional forms and received a £10 bonus. The one-year contract entitled me to £2 10s per match or £5 per first team match. I could not believe my luck. If I had not been expelled, I would not have been spotted, but that's life and for me, it worked out.

The manager at Leeds was Billy Hampson. I must have made a quick impression for Leeds United's nursery team, Headingley Rangers, because within weeks, after scoring a hat-trick for the reserves, I made my first team debut in a midweek fixture at Charlton Athletic. I was 18 and came in for first choice centre-forward George Ainsley, who had flu.

Leeds lost 5-0, but I learned some valuable lessons. At our first corner kick, I was looking at the ball when Don Welsh came up behind me and slipped my shorts down. He knew I was a young lad and said, "you will remember to be more aware next time!" Charlton's goalkeeper, Sam Bartram, had a great reputation and was on top form that day. It was tough, but I went close with a couple of headers. This would be my only first team game during the season, which was the first full Football League season after World War II. Leeds had an old squad and experienced their worst-ever season, winning just six games.

When Billy Hampson resigned with a few games remaining, relegation was already a certainty. Willis Edwards, who assisted trainer Box Roxburgh, took over and began to replace older players in addition to working on our fitness levels. Willis had captained both Leeds United and England in the late 1920s. He was a marvellous footballer in his day, but as a manager Willis was quiet. In the 1947/48 season I continued playing in the

Central League for the reserves, but could only train on evenings as I did my national service with the 'Bevin Boys' at Middleton colliery during the day.

Before the 1948/49 season started, Major Frank Buckley became the manager. He was a very different character to Willis and life was never dull with the Major, who was in his early 60s and immediately made his presence felt. Major Buckley had been the driving force behind Wolves' pre-war transformation from a poor Second Division side to one of the best teams in the country and the Leeds board hoped he could make a similar impact at Elland Road. He had also spotted a young lad called Billy Wright and signed him to Molineux.

By now, I had completed my national service and soon got another first team opportunity. In my first game back, I scored in a 1-1 draw at Barnsley and struck again a week later on my home debut when we defeated Grimsby 6-3. We deserved the points with a great display of attacking football. The match was played in a great spirit. The only complaints came from both goalkeepers due to poor defending.

I kept my place in the side and had my first experience of playing in a packed festive programme. On Christmas Day, I scored in a 3-2 defeat at West Ham United. We faced the Hammers again on Boxing Day at home, so Major Buckley insisted we stayed overnight at a Sheffield hotel. Some players were not happy, but he wanted us to rest. We lost 3-1. Nevertheless, we went on to enjoy four-goal home wins over Bradford and Barnsley later in the season. Apart from scoring two goals in each game, our 4-2 victory over Bradford was unforgettable because we played in blizzard conditions, which was really tough.

We finished just below halfway in the table, which was disappointing, but not as humiliating as a FA Cup third round defeat to Newport County at Elland Road. Newport were bottom of Division 3 (South), so going out to them was embarrassing. I scored early on with a shot that crashed in off the bar, but Newport, inspired by winger Harold Williams, fought back to beat us 3-1. Our defeat was truly put into perspective when Notts County defeated Newport 11-0 a week later in a league match.

Newport aside, the season had gone well for me personally, as I ended the campaign top scorer with 14 goals. Whatever the result, Leeds fans were always fair with the players and very enthusiastic. Like all sides of that era, Leeds played the W-M formation and always tried to attack, but it was hard work in the Second Division as we faced useful sides such as Tottenham Hotspur, Sheffield United, Sheffield Wednesday and Southampton.

During the close season, our FA Cup tormentor, Harold Williams, arrived at Elland Road. His performance had clearly impressed the club directors. Joining Leeds enabled Harold to link up again with John Charles as they had been on the ground staff together at Swansea Town. Major Buckley signed John during the campaign and quickly gave him a first team debut. John was only 16, but it was clear he had massive potential.

The team was developing and there was terrific banter between the players in the dressing room. When I first arrived, Tom Holley was the Mickey-taker. Tom was a stalwart of the team and before a game would joke, "if the ball goes past me the centre-forward doesn't." George Ainsley took over from Tom as chief Mickey-taker and was a real comedian. He got everyone going. Both picked on David Cochrane, who was only small, so had to take a lot of good-natured stick.

Major Buckley was a real personality, a disciplinarian. You could not get away with anything. The Major was also an innovator and tried everything in training to make us a better team. Much was stamina-based, especially during pre-season. We had a local run to Morley and back down the Huddersfield Road. It was very hard. Facilities were basic at the club, but Major Buckley insisted we had to train often on the car park so we didn't ruin the pitch for a match.

We had a shooting pen, which I had never seen before. We also had a running track under the main stands for sprinting. We hung footballs from a beam to improve our jumping ability. The Major also used to put two bricks either side of a football. When you kicked the ball he would say, "that will keep your eye on the ball!" We used gym shoes in training for this exercise. I actually hit the brick once and it really hurt. I concentrated fully after that misjudgement. We also had a kicking machine installed, where balls came out at different speeds and heights. The machine simulated corner kicks and passes, which helped improve our heading, trapping, volleying and trapping. It also sharpened the goalkeeper's reflexes.

At Wolves, Major Buckley had caused headlines when he gave some of his players monkey gland extract to 'sharpen their thinking' in their run to the 1939 FA Cup final. We had a more advanced form of 'Pick Me up'. We took pills that pepped us up, but you did feel low afterwards. In training, the Major would scream at us through a loudhailer. He didn't mince his words and before a game always geed us up.

Although a taskmaster, Major Buckley looked after all the players. I enjoyed playing in London especially and we always stayed at the Great Northern Hotel. Before one match, as a surprise, Major Buckley organised for us to see British heavyweight champion Bruce Woodcock fight at Haringey Arena. Unfortunately, the hotel was a room short, so Major Buckley arranged for a taxi to take John Charles and myself to another hotel. We could not believe it when the taxi pulled up at the Mayfair Hotel. It was the biggest in London. We were the two youngest players in the team and felt completely out of our depth at this prestigious hotel. The porter asked us both for our luggage, but we hardly had anything. We were then given a suite of rooms. It was unbelievable. Neither of us had never seen anything like it before and didn't dare stay for breakfast. In the morning, we went straight back to the team hotel to eat with the boys and tell everyone of our experience. Life was great and we were all part of the local community. Many of us lived close to Elland Road and often attended supporter's club functions.

During the 1949/50 season, after a poor start, I scored in a 1-0 win at Sheffield United and 2-0 victory at home to Cardiff City. During the festive period, I opened the scoring in a 3-1 win over Preston North End on Christmas Eve. The win against Preston sparked a great period of form for us as we climbed the league table courtesy of six consecutive victories.

During a memorable run, I struck the winner at Swansea Town on New Year's Eve. I found the target at Coventry City in a 4-0 triumph and then hit the opening goal during a 2-1 over Luton Town at Elland Road. We also enjoyed a brilliant 3-0 win over title favourites Tottenham Hotspur and then defeated Southampton courtesy of a Harold Williams strike. I had an assist in Harold's goal.

In the midst of this run of form, we embarked on our FA Cup campaign in confident mood, but nobody tipped us to cause a major shock despite our fantastic form. But we duly confounded everyone.

Our third round clash at Division 3 (North) side Carlisle United was notable only in that it was a potential giant-killing clash for Carlisle. The fixture caught the imagination of local supporters as an attendance of almost 23,000 packed Brunton Park hoping for a cup upset. They would soon be disappointed as I opened the scoring inside five minutes by controlling a through ball before firing home.

The goal stunned Carlisle. Bill Shankly was at the start of his managerial career, but could not counter tactically the threat of Eddie McMorran in a deep-lying role. Frank Dudley with two goals, Harold Williams and David Cochrane completed our first half domination, though we conceded a goal before half-time. If we had continued at the same pace, we would have racked up a record club score.

Amazingly, just as we expected praise for our display, in the dressing room, Major Buckley did nothing but moan about Carlisle's goal and went back to Leeds before the second half started. We could not believe it because it had been a tremendous attacking performance in the opening 45 minutes. The Major was a one off as a manager though, so his bizarre reaction should not have come as a surprise. The second half was never going to match the first and the match finished 5-2.

The fourth round draw gave us a terrific tie against Bolton Wanderers at Elland Road and guaranteed a capacity attendance. Bolton were a top First Division side with household names such as Nat Lofthouse, Tommy Banks, Malcolm Barrass and Willie Moir playing for them. It would be a tough encounter. Before the match, we warmed up against Tottenham and achieved a tremendous result. The clash against the Londoners, who would win the Second Division title at the end of this season and claim the First Division championship a year later, was a game that I have always remembered because of both our performance and the difficulties I experienced just getting to the game. All the local buses were full due to supporters flocking to see the league leaders. I had to run all the way from East End Park to catch a tram. For a professional footballer life was very different to the modern day superstars. There was a long queue when I finally made it to the trams and I only just made the game.

A crowd of over 50,000 packed into Elland Road. Reporters noted that it was our best performance in post-war football and it was difficult to disagree because we played some great football. Tommy Burden and Eric Kerfoot dominated opponents, while John Charles had centre-forward Len Duquemin in his pocket. David Cochrane and Ray Iggledon struck our goals in a 3-0 win. We were ready for Bolton.

We had developed a useful side. Harry Searson was a steady goalkeeper, Jimmy Dunn was a solid full-back, Jim Milburn had tremendous power and took free-kicks. Jim McCabe was ever reliable, while captain Tommy Burden was a smashing chap. David Cochrane and Harold Williams were both very tricky wingers; Ray Iggledon was rock solid, Frank Dudley very fast and, of course, we also had John Charles in defence.

John was a marvellous player; we played up front together just once when he filled in as an emergency striker, but got in each other's way. John and I were good friends. When he played for Juventus, John entertained my wife Mollie, who I married in 1951, and I. John was always a tremendous host. On the field, John never seemed in a hurry; he played the game at his pace and was always at ease. John never dashed about; he positioned himself well so didn't have to worry. John was a natural footballer and, of course, went on to become a prolific goalscorer for both Leeds and Juventus.

Demand for cup tickets was unprecedented for Leeds United, which forced directors to make the Bolton match all-ticket for the first time at Elland Road. When tickets went on sale a week earlier, on the day we beat Southampton, anxious supporters quickly bought them as cup fever struck the club. All the talk throughout the week centred on the Bolton match. When we ran out there was an electric atmosphere as over 51,000 crammed into the ground.

The conditions were terrible because the pitch was frozen. We wore special boots and kneepads. but still found it difficult to stand up while Bolton, Lofthouse and all, kept their feet and dominated possession. Nevertheless, against the run of play, Harold Williams gave us a first half lead after being set up by David Cochrane. I was struggling to get the better of centre-half Matt Gillies, while Nat gave John Charles a torrid time, but Tommy Burden, Jimmy Dunn and Jim Milburn defended brilliantly.

An equaliser had to come and after Nat had struck the woodwork twice, forced Harry Searson into a number of saves and Jimmy Dunn to clear a goal-bound effort off the line, he scored with a close-range shot. To neutral observers Bolton must have been favourites to progress, but we dug deep and eventually held on for a commendable draw. We felt satisfied in the dressing room afterwards and, though tired, looked forward to the replay despite knowing we would be huge underdogs.

We had enjoyed a fine result and four days later found ourselves crossing the Pennines for the biggest game many of us had ever faced, hoping to win the replay. In reality, I feared the worst and did not expect to come out on top against a crack First Division side, especially away from home. However, football has always had the habit of providing shock results, so there was a chance. Whatever was before us I knew we would go out believing in our ability to win and though nervous, we did not feel overawed. Playing in front of a capacity crowd had inspired us and would do so again.

As in the first game, the pitch was barely playable, which would level things up slightly and there were doubts if it would pass the referee's pitch inspection but it did. On the night, we were fired up and made the perfect start when Frank Dudley headed home Harold Williams pinpoint cross on just two minutes. John Charles countered the threat of Nat Lofthouse and we battled through to half-time a goal ahead.

On the resumption, we again made a great start and this time I headed a goal in to put us 2-0 in front. Matt Gillies marked me as in the first encounter and we had a great tussle, but I got the better of him in this attack. We were all jubilant, but Bolton rocked us back within a few minutes when Nat set up Harry McShane to score neatly past Harry Searson. We had to dig deep again and kept Bolton at bay, but 20 minutes from time, Nat thumped in a great strike to level the scores at 2-2.

As in the first game, Bolton were favourites after coming from behind again, but we held firm until full-time. Major Buckley did not come out. Bob Roxburgh did and gave us a few words of encouragement. It was down to us now and we had to steel ourselves for extra-time. Whether Bolton relaxed, I'm unsure, but inside five minutes of the first extra period, I headed on a deep free-kick from John Charles and Frank crashed the ball home in off the crossbar. The goal proved to be the winner despite constant Bolton pressure.

At the final whistle, it was a marvellous feeling and back in the dressing room, we were all so excited. We felt on top of the world because we had beaten a classy team in the most prestigious knockout competition of all. Major Buckley told the media that it was the best performance he had witnessed, which was some accolade.

Cup fever was gripping the city of Leeds as we awaited Cardiff City in the next round. An FA Cup mascot doll called Lulu was embraced, and as in the previous round, club directors had a problem because of the demand for tickets. This game was seen as the biggest in the club's history as Leeds had never reached the last eight of the FA Cup before.

We went into the game on the back of a 4-0 win at Coventry when I scored one of our goals and 20,000 fans attended a reserve game at Elland Road as cup tickets were on sale. During the week leading up to the Cardiff game, our win at Bolton was still a major talking point and in the Cardiff programme notes the editor described the match as 'slush-cum-water-cum-ice-ballet'! Our focus though was on the match in hand and a crowd of over 53,000 packed Elland Road for a clash that only just avoided being postponed due to heavy rain.

Radio star Wilfred Pickles provided pre-match entertainment and we made the perfect start with goals by Harold Williams and David Cochrane inside 10 minutes. Cardiff reduced the deficit to a single goal, but once Ray Iggledon scored in the second half, we knew that first ever quarter-final place was ours.

We had created club history and now faced mighty Arsenal at Highbury for a place in the semi-finals. During the build up, papers were full of stories. It was the best thing that had happened to the club for years and 150 coaches made the journey to London. We travelled down the day before the big match by train. We had a private carriage and stayed overnight as usual at the Great Northern Hotel, although there was no special transfer for John Charles and myself this time.

During the build up we'd defeated Luton and lost at Cardiff in the league, but all attention now was on the FA Cup. Highbury was at the time one of the best grounds in the country. Only four of our team had played at the stadium. Before the game, Arsenal's double international [Football and Cricket] Denis Compton said to John Charles and me, "you've never been here before?", so he showed us around. He was a smashing chap. Arsenal had a great team that included the Compton brothers, Denis and Leslie, Wales goalkeeper George Swindin and England international half-back Joe Mercer.

We had lost just two games in four months, so felt confident despite having to face a top-class Division 1 side. In front of over 63,000 fans, we played really well. Leslie Compton marked me; we had a great battle. The referee had a reputation for wanting to be the star of a game and from the kick-off seemed pro-Arsenal. Every decision seemed to go their way. It was a great game, though, and we could have won, but they snatched a second half goal when Lewis toe-poked the ball into the net. After the goal, Arsenal hung on for victory as Frank Dudley and Ray Iggledon went agonisingly close to equalising.

We were not disgraced in defeat at all. Arsenal had the luck with them. I really enjoyed the encounter and it was great facing top stars of the day. We had tremendous support and it was a memorable occasion. Major Buckley was convinced that we could win the Cup. We were really disappointed and felt that we should have beaten Arsenal, who went on to defeat Liverpool in the final. It would have been fantastic to reach Wembley, and we had very nearly caused another major upset, but it wasn't to be.

In the league, we suffered a bit of a cup hangover. Our form stuttered and although we were thereabouts, we struggled to win games. I missed the final few matches of the season. Two victories in the final week brought us a fifth place finish, which though a shade disappointing was an improvement on recent seasons.

During a post-season tour of Holland, we won two out of four games. I kept a log for the Yorkshire Evening News. On the Channel crossing most of us played cards and after a lucky half-hour Frank Dudley's chief worry was how to get his winnings through customs, as he had more than the maximum amount allowed by visitors. The secretary of the Dutch FA greeted us at the Hook of Holland. He said the Dutch were hoping to gain tactical skills by visits of British teams. How times have changed.

The Dutch played a different game to us. They didn't hold onto the ball, not even if they were being harassed. They always looked to pass the ball and keep it moving towards the opponent's goal. Unlike in England, goal-keepers were helped by the continental rule that a goalkeeper could not be charged and another point of difference was the way crowds left their seats at half-time and walked around the cinder track in an orderly parade. During the tour, we were also deeply impressed when visiting the site of the battle of Arnhem. We observed a moment's silence when Tommy Burden laid a memorial wreath.

During the 1950/51 campaign, once again, I finished top scorer and we enjoyed some terrific results. I got off to a flyer with a goal in an opening day victory over Doncaster Rovers and struck in wins against Coventry City, Luton Town, Chesterfield and Birmingham City. Following a thrilling 4-4 draw at Doncaster, I scored both goals in a 2-0 Boxing Day victory against West Ham before grabbing my only Leeds hat-trick in a great 5-3 win against Southampton. I went in at half-time feeling happy with myself, but Major Buckley played pop with me for scoring with my wrong foot. He had been a centre-half in his playing days and said I would not have scored past him because I let the ball come across me before hitting it.

In the FA Cup, we looked forward to another good run, but it wasn't to be. After defeating Middlesbrough, Major Buckley had the idea of rubbing whisky on us before facing Manchester United. Before we knew it, we were four goals down. United's centre-half said to me, "Are you lot drunk? You smell like it." We kept it down to 4-0.

I missed much of the run-in, but scored in the final game when we defeated Swansea Town to finish fifth for a second successive season. It was disappointing as were only four points behind runners-up Manchester City.

During a post-season tour to Eire, we had a fantastic welcome in Dublin and our headquarters at the Gresham Hotel was painted in blue and gold. The food was first class. Back in Leeds we still had an 8d meat ration while here the steaks almost covered the plate. Our biggest trouble was a shortage of cash because the shops were full of things we wanted. Most of us quickly spent our allowance, so kept away from the shops and took to the golf course. The monotony of long journeys through lovely countryside and quaint villages was relieved by the mouth-organ wizardry of Ernie "Larry Adler" Stephenson.

The coming campaign would prove to be my last for Leeds United. I scored on the opening day in a 1-1 against Brentford and struck two in a 3-1 victory against Sheffield United, however after a defeat at Barnsley I was on my way out of Elland Road to Bramall Lane. Controversy raged in local newspapers. It was not surprising as Leeds had included at different times Henry, Ainsley, Short, Wakefield, Clarke, Dudley, Frost and myself at centre-forward.

I was sad to leave Leeds, but Frank Fidler had been signed to replace me. I didn't ask for a transfer, but Sheffield United came in, so it was time to move on. Frank didn't play many games and within a year John Charles showed his ability in attack and versatility to switch from central defence. I faced John just once before he switched positions and we had a great tussle, when Sheffield came out on top, winning 3-0 at Elland Road. In 1952/53 while John crashed in goals galore for Leeds United, Sheffield United won the Division 2 title, but within a few months of the new First Division campaign, I contracted tuberculosis, which ended my league career.

Of course, it was not the end that I'd planned, but I had a host of great memories to look back on, especially Leeds United's FA Cup run in 1950. The Arsenal game was one that got away, but our victory at Bolton was an epic match and the toughest of my career. We knocked out one of the game's top sides and richly deserved our victory. It was a match I'll never forget and the best result I experienced for the club.

PAUL REANEY
RIGHT-BACK 1961–1978

BORN   22nd October 1944, London
SIGNED   October 1961 as apprentice
LEEDS CAREER   748 games, 9 goals
HONOURS   2 Division One Championships, 1 Division Two Championship, 1 FA Cup, 1 League Cup, 2 Fairs Cups, 3 England caps, 5 England U23 caps
LEFT   Free transfer to Bradford City, June 1978

Paul possessed lightning pace. 'Speedy' Reaney was a strong tackler, superb man-marker and had great positional awareness at right-back. Super fit, athletic, a fine crosser of the ball and renowned for his goal-line clearances, Paul was a member of teams that won numerous major honours for Leeds United during the Revie era, but a broken leg cost him an FA Cup final place and a chance to play at the World Cup finals in Mexico. Paul is one of only five players to make over 700 appearances for Leeds.

Leeds United 1 v Manchester United 0

FA Cup Semi-final replay
Wednesday 31st March 1965

City Ground
Attendance 46,300

Leeds United reach the FA Cup final for the first time in their history.

Teams

Don Revie	Managers	Matt Busby
Gary Sprake	1	Pat Dunne
Paul Reaney	2	Shay Brennan
Willie Bell	3	Tony Dunne
Billy Bremner	4	Pat Crerand
Jack Charlton	5	Bill Foulkes
Norman Hunter	6	Nobby Stiles
Johnny Giles	7	John Connelly
Jim Storrie	8	Bobby Charlton
Alan Peacock	9	David Herd
Bobby Collins	10	Denis Law
Terry Cooper	11	George Best
Bremner 88	**Scorers**	

Referee: R Windle

"I PLAYED OVER 700 games for Leeds United. My debut against Swansea Town back in 1962 will always be special to me, along with many big games we played in our battle for honours over the years. But to choose one? Well, winning the FA Cup semi-final against Manchester United in 1965 was fantastic. My initial thought at the time was, "we're at Wembley, I've achieved one of my big ambitions already." I'd watched the FA Cup final since I was 10 years old, now I was playing in a showpiece final. I could look ahead to playing on the biggest stage in football.

I was born in Fulham, but moved to Leeds when I was a few weeks old. I attended Cross Green School and participated in most sports. Running was my main strength. I raced over 100 yards as it was in those days, and enjoyed some success. Local schools competed against each other and we had finals at Roundhay Park.

I remember racing regularly against Paul Madeley, who went to Parkside Secondary School. Paul was a fantastic runner and I failed to beat him in the big races because he was so quick. I did eventually defeat him in a semi-final race one year at Temple Newsam, but only because I wore my tracksuit bottoms and he didn't. It was a cool night and I won by a few yards. I was pleased, but that was my sole victory because as usual Paul won the final.

Away from sprinting, I played football for Middleton Parkside Juniors with Paul, Kevin Hector and Rod Johnson. We won trophies most years. I also followed the fortunes of Leeds United. After playing on a Saturday morning, I watched matches at Elland Road from the terraces in the late 50s and early 60s when Don Revie, Jack Charlton and Billy Bremner played.

I gained selection for Leeds City Boys, but it was not until I was invited to Elland Road for trials by a Leeds United scout that I really wanted to become a footballer. It wasn't an academy as clubs have nowadays. One of the club's coaches, Syd Owen, used to take the training sessions on a Tuesday and Thursday night. Around 30 teenagers came from Leeds, Bradford, Halifax and Huddersfield hoping to make it. Following six or seven sessions, I was asked to join the ground staff.

Leeds United manager Jack Taylor was all set to sign me as an apprentice professional, but lost his job. Things were briefly uncertain as to whether I'd still join, but Don Revie was appointed as the new manager and duly signed me. Before joining Leeds I was an apprentice motor mechanic at Appleyard's earning £1 9d a week. At Leeds, I was earning £12 a week. I thought I'd won the pools. I was living at home, so it was nice to give some extra money to my parents. I was just 17 and on good money, but had to work hard. The set up at Leeds was very different to how it is today. There was no training facility like Thorp Arch. We went to the ground every day, rather than travelled there for matches, and trained on Fullerton Park, which is now a car park.

On my first day as an apprentice, I was kitted out in my white kit, but my first duty was to clean the toilets. Being an apprentice was character-building and generated a bond between the young players trying to make the grade. There was no machinery for ground maintenance. I used to dig out weeds by hand, but then landed a good job in the dressing room looking after the kit, then cleaning out the bath, dressing room and medical room. My favourite job was cleaning the football boots, changing the studs and keeping them clean because that was my trade. Combining training with our duties was tough but good for us.

Other youngsters on the ground staff included Rod Johnson, Gary Sprake, Norman Hunter and Terry Cooper. Paul Madeley joined a few months after me and kept his sprinting ability right through his career. It was no effort for him and that is how he got the nickname 'Rolls Royce'. He purred along! Other youngsters to make an impression included the likes of Jimmy Greenhoff, Peter Lorimer, David Harvey, Terry Hibbitt, Rod Belfitt and Mick Bates.

Whether Don Revie made an immediate impact was hard to say because, as ground staff lads, we were playing in the youth team, so didn't know what it was like for first team players. Don brought us up so we understood what he wanted. Training took place with Syd, Les Cocker, Cyril Partridge and Bob English. We enjoyed some success and won a youth tournament.

Club captain was Bobby Collins, who starred for Celtic in the 1950s before playing for Everton. Bobby saved the club from going down when he joined towards the end of the 1961/62 season and immediately made a massive impact on the apprentices. Bobby took me under his wing on and off the park. He also put me straight on certain things, especially the art of tackling. We were taught how to tackle to hurt, not to maim. There is a difference. You tackle hard to put your opponent off, not to break a leg. Bobby was the type of person that we all looked up to; he had done it all before. Bobby was only five foot four inches tall, but what a hard player. He could look after himself.

We'd all trained together from the early days, so as you moved into the first team set up, training was pepped up from what you were used to doing. It was more aggressive and, depending on when we had matches, influenced how hard we trained. If we didn't have a midweek game, which was rare, then it was hard training early in the week as we built up to a weekend match. If you trained too hard you could lose sharpness for a game, so it was a balancing act.

Training was always competitive because we were young kids aiming to break through. We did as we were told and if we were good enough a chance would come. I worked on my weaker left foot and made sure that if I didn't win the ball my opponent didn't either. With me, it was a question of working constantly on my game to improve. We all kept our feet on the ground. If anyone became a bit lazy, the other players would let you know.

I came to the club as a centre-half. Syd Owen liked me in that position because I could cover both full-backs, but the gaffer said early on that my speed and mobility would make the team more effective out wide, so I switched to right back. My dad wasn't happy with the change and went to see the gaffer, but Don said, "give Paul a month." After a month, my dad apologised because the gaffer was right.

When I received my first team debut against Swansea Town in September 1962 it was a shock because I'd only played a few games in the Central League for the reserve side. Pundits today say that kids play too many games. When I started, Leeds United had an 'A', 'B', intermediate, reserve and first team. Often we'd play for the juniors in a morning then the 'A' or 'B' team in the afternoon. There was a lot of football, but that has changed.

The first team was not playing well and sat near the bottom of the Second Division, Don decided to make major changes. The gaffer pulled me in and said, "you'll be travelling down to Swansea along with Norman Hunter, Rod Johnson and Gary Sprake." I told my parents that I was going to Swansea. They were delighted, but could also not believe an opportunity had come so quickly. I was still only 17. My dad travelled down to watch the game and I was not the only one to get my big break. Gary had played just once and replaced Tommy Younger, Norman came in for Freddie Goodwin, Rod deputised for John Charles, who wasn't feeling well, while I took over from Grenville Hair.

Grenville had been a fantastic servant to Leeds. Although he must have been disappointed that he was going to lose his place, as I got on the coach for the match at Swansea he came over to me and said, "Paul, all the best, its your turn now. I've had my day." That was great and said a lot about Grenville. We won 2-0, Rod and Billy Bremner scored.

Apart from Rod, we all kept our place for a home debut at home to Chelsea, who were going well and would gain promotion along with Stoke City. Pundits predicted we'd get a hiding. After 10 minutes, Eric Smith slipped and broke his leg. Of course, with no substitutes available back then, we were up against it and playing a very good side, but we came off to a standing ovation after winning 2-0. Albert Johanesson scored both goals. We felt like we had won the Cup.

We were young, ambitious and the results began to come. We moved up the league and fans took us to their hearts. Gary, Norman and I kept our places in the team and you could sense from the crowd and write ups in the local press that things were developing at Elland Road. We ended the season in fifth place, which gave us confidence for the 1963/64 campaign.

Arriving at Leeds United when I did was a good time because the side was getting older and struggling. I didn't come into the team thinking, right I must stay in the side. I thought, play to your ability and if you are good enough then you'll stay in. That is what happened.

During the 1962/63 campaign, I began gaining a reputation for clearing the ball off the line. The gaffer didn't tell me to drop back, it just developed. One day Don asked me why I did it. I told him that when someone was about to take a shot from 20 yards and I was 15 yards away by the time I got anywhere near him, I was in no-man's land. To me, I had more chance of getting back on the goal-line to stop an effort on target if the keeper missed it. The gaffer agreed and it went from there.Now everyone seems to remember me for it.

Change was occurring at the club as the gaffer's influence took hold. There was a clear shift in ethos and professionalism. There was also a closer relationship between the players and supporters than there is today. Every Friday, before a Saturday game at Elland Road, I used to go shopping for my wife in Leeds market. Fans used to tap me on the shoulder as I queued for fruit and vegetables to wish the team and myself luck. There was no bodyguards, no security. We travelled all over to attend supporter's clubs events. We mingled with fans and it carried on like that throughout my career at the club.

I remember distinctly the gaffer's pre-season talk before the 1963/64 Division Two campaign. It would be the same every season for a decade. He said we are going for every trophy. In those days, as well as the three major domestic competitions, we also played in the West Riding Senior Cup against teams like Bradford Park Avenue, Halifax Town and Huddersfield Town. Even then, Don would play his strongest side. For the gaffer if you didn't win a trophy it was a bad season. That campaign we won two trophies, the Second Division title and West Riding Cup. That was one hell of a season at that stage for us and it saw us develop a winning mentality. During the campaign, Johnny Giles and Alan Peacock strengthened the team. Gilesy was superb, especially when he later teamed up with Billy. How Manchester United let him go, I don't know.

The Second Division was a tough league with the likes of Preston, Sunderland and Manchester City. At times, we were not pretty to watch. We'd get a goal up and keep possession. We'd be booed, but needed to dig in for a result. It was physical at times and we brought that into our game against First Division sides. We could play football, but when required could mix it as well. There was a true team spirit. If one of us had an off day, the gaffer would not drop you. He knew we'd bounce back. If someone was having a tough time, then you would get more from other players. The lads would give you encouragement. Team spirit was incredible.

We quickly developed a reputation for being a hard, physical side. Teams discovered that at Elland Road, you would generally go home with a few bruises and no points. Some clubs found that intimidating. If a winger went past me and it was the side where the gaffer was, he'd look at me and I'd know that he must not go past me again. We got a bad press, but it was a bit harsh and we were not the only team that gave opponents a tough time.

During our first season back in top-flight football, 1964/65, teams initially underestimated us. They did not realise just how good a side we actually were, but they soon discovered what Leeds United was all about. We knew that we would be competitive and were not in awe of anybody. That was down to Don Revie. The gaffer wanted Elland Road to be a fortress. He told us when opponents saw the sign for Leeds on the motorway, he wanted them to tremble. We didn't win every game we played at home, but opponents always knew they would be in for a hard match. The gaffer brought us up not to fear any of the top sides like Liverpool, Manchester United, Arsenal, Tottenham Hotspur, Everton or Chelsea.

Because we could battle and would not get intimidated, it did not surprise me that we picked up great wins at Everton, Manchester United and Arsenal in that first season in the First Division. All were memorable clashes. At Goodison Park, the referee had to take both sides off the pitch to cool down, while at Old Trafford, Manchester United wanted the referee to abandon the game due to worsening fog late on, but he refused. When we travelled down to London it was always important to put on a display, our win at Highbury earned us a double over the Gunners.

At Anfield, we lost 2-1, but won our home clash 4-2. Both games took place early in the season. There was great respect between the sides and our matches against Bill Shankly's men were games when you took no prisoners. Bill and Don were firm friends, but, when we played, both sides were desperate to win. Our clashes became great battles each season.

By New Year, we were battling away at the top alongside Manchester United and Chelsea when the FA Cup came around. I always looked forward to playing in the competition because of its history and now we had a side capable of going a long way. Of course, reaching Wembley, which was something Leeds United had never done, was a key target for us all. When I started out as a professional footballer, I wanted to win the First Division championship, FA Cup, any other tournaments we competed in and represent England. At Leeds United, we grew up wanting to be medal winners. That is how great sides are judged.

Our FA Cup run saw us defeat Southport, Everton, Shrewsbury Town and Crystal Palace to reach the semi-finals, making us the first side in the club's history to make the last four. The wins over Southport, Shrewsbury and Palace were comfortable, but our clash with Everton in the fourth round was a much tougher affair. We'd gone out to them the previous season in a replay and were determined to go one better this time.

There was definitely an edge to games against Everton, probably because of Bobby Collins' link with the club as he'd spent four years there before joining Leeds, and after drawing 1-1 at home we edged the replay 2-1 following goals by Jack Charlton and Don Weston. It was a night when Bobby and Gary Sprake excelled. We were not too popular with opposing fans, especially those toffee supporters at Everton. Police had to escort us away from Goodison Park. After this game, and others in the future, we had to lay down on the coach floor with the curtains drawn because opposing fans smashed the windows. We always had a smile on our faces though, because we'd got a result.

Missing that night was Albert Johannesson. On his day, especially at home, Albert was tremendous and had great ball skill and speed, but he didn't tend to like the physical side of the game. When we faced a particularly tough battle, it was not in his makeup and the gaffer would sometimes select Terry Cooper. Terry also played in the 3-0 win at Palace. The clash was close for an hour or so until Alan Peacock, back in the side after two knee operations, scored our opening goal. Alan was an international player and had proved a good signing in our promotion year, but injuries were catching up with him. He would play just one more season.

We were a game away from one of my big ambitions, to play in an FA Cup final at Wembley. For players and supporters it was a tremendous time. Cup fever gripped the club and fans were desperate for tickets. The queues were incredible at the ticket office. The club had never experienced anything like it before. We had enjoyed a brilliant season. We were going well in the First Division and now potentially had an FA Cup final to look forward to playing. Pundits were suddenly talking about a 'double' in our first season, which was quite incredible from where we were the previous season, fighting for promotion. We didn't realise just how big the double was, but the city was buzzing. Leeds United was definitely on the football map.

The anticipation built and built as we approached the semi-final. We warmed up with comprehensive home victories over Burnley [5-1] and Fulham [4-1] to keep the momentum going. Albert was on fire, scoring in both games, and gained selection for the semi-final clash with Manchester United, while Liverpool and Chelsea took on each other in the other game.

This was my first semi-final and I was nervous. Manchester United had seen it all before. They had won the Cup in 1963 and got to the semi-final in 1964 when they lost to eventual winners West Ham United – but for us it was all new. The build up was like no game we'd experienced in terms of media coverage. It was a huge match.

It could not have been much tougher as we took on our rivals for the title. We had won 1-0 at Old Trafford earlier in the season, but that now counted for nothing. Facing Manchester United was not physically as hard like some games, but it was extremely tough because they had dangerous players such as Bobby Charlton, Denis Law and George Best, who was just breaking onto the scene and making a massive impact on the game.

The stage was set for a showdown at Sheffield Wednesday's Hillsborough ground, but the clash ended up as a bad-tempered 0-0 draw. The match was played on an extremely muddy pitch. There were far too many fouls, mainly by Manchester United, to make it an open game.

Nobby Stiles and Denis Law were booked. There was one scuffle involving six players and Albert Johanesson suffered damaged ligaments following a terrible challenge by Stiles.

On such a surface good football was impossible and for me that game ranks as the worst FA Cup semi-final I played in. The conditions put both sides off. It was almost impossible to turn. The ball stuck in the mud and chances were scarce. It was a dour game and the referee, Mr Windle, received a lot of stick in the press.

We hoped for a better contest at Nottingham Forest's City Ground in the replay, which would decide who would face Liverpool at Wembley following their victory over Chelsea. The chances were good because the surface was fast and dry compared to the Hillsborough mud-heap. With Albert injured, Terry Cooper deputised. There were no other changes to either side.

As in the first game I man-marked Bestie. The rest of the lads lined up as normal, but had to be aware, especially Big Jack, Norman Hunter and Willie Bell, because there may be nobody at right-back if George wandered about to get rid of me. In the gaffer's pre-match dossier notes, Don always made reference to this, not that we would forget, but he wanted to make sure we knew every player's strengths and weaknesses.

We normally played a flat back four on a sort of swivel system. We'd all cover each other, if the ball was on Willie's side (later Terry Cooper), I would move slightly inside and be the last man. We'd have Willie, Norman a little deeper, Jack a little deeper and finally myself. If the ball was played to the left-winger, Willie would be last man in the covering position and I would take on my man.

The gaffer changed this, though, against Manchester United, although it would lose part of my game, in an attempt to stop Bestie. There was no choice because George could destroy a team on his own, so we had to nullify him. Stopping Bestie made the game in effect 10-a-side. My speed allowed me to keep up with George and avoid buying his dummies. My speed also gave me a chance to get back if he ever got past me. Retrieving a situation was something I worked on in training. I'd start from a bottom position and there were techniques that helped me get up quickly and back.

Marking Bestie, my concentration had to be strong, as I had to stick to him like glue. Over the years, it became a mental game. George would know exactly where I'd be every game, on his heels tracking him and on occasion it did get physical. We had many great tussles. I remember George scoring during a clash at Old Trafford in the 1965/66 season. He laughed at me. "I've got one over on you today." I had the last laugh though because I got our equaliser. I only scored nine in my Leeds career, so I remember them all. The following season, I scored our opening goal in a 3-1 win, which was even sweeter, but I knew my role in this fixture. Often I would not get many touches, but it benefited the side and that's what we were all about.

Manchester United enjoyed the better of the opening half in terms of possession, but created nothing clear-cut, though Bestie and John Connelly did their best to carve out the chances. We almost took the lead through a Big Jack header, but Tony Dunne was on hand to clear off the line. Mostly we were on the defensive. Willie, Norman and myself stood firm, but we were mainly indebted to Big Jack, who was immense in the heart of our defence. As a spectacle, it was a far better match than at Hillsborough. There were fewer tackles flying in and the match was more open. The referee Mr Windle also handled this game far better.

In the second half, chances eventually came Manchester United's way. Gary Sprake did brilliantly to stop headers by Bobby Charlton and Bestie, before coming to our rescue again to deny strikes by Denis Law and David Herd. Charlton and Herd both hit the side netting, but as the game entered the last 20 minutes, we came into the match.

Don switched things around. Johnny Giles, who was on the right wing, pulled back into Billy's midfield position, Jim Storrie moved from inside-forward to accommodate Johnny, while Billy joined the attack from his midfield position. The gaffer's changes worked as we finally enjoyed pressure through a number of corners and free-kick's.

Big Jack went agonisingly close with a header and keeper Pat Dunne had to turn the ball behind on three occasions when under severe pressure. We sensed that a goal would come. Finally, with the match locked at 0-0 and seemingly destined for extra-time, we struck with just two minutes remaining on the clock.

Billy scored the all-important goal. The breakthrough came when Nobby Stiles fouled him near the halfway line. From the resultant free-kick, Billy twisted before back-heading Johnny Giles' floated free-kick into the roof of the net past Pat Dunne. We were all ecstatic. There was barely enough time for Manchester United to get back into the game.

Billy's effort was no one-off as he proved over the coming years to have a knack of scoring important semi-final goals. His strikes would see us through two FA Cup, a Fairs Cup and European Cup semi-finals. It wasn't just cup games, though, when Billy came up trumps. If we needed some-thing, Don would not hesitate to push Billy up and often he did it off his own back. We'd be ready to cover his runs. Someone would yell, "Billy's gone again," and drop back.

At the final whistle, Leeds supporters invaded the pitch to celebrate. Back in the dressing room, everyone was ecstatic, but we were also hugely relieved because we had withstood a lot of pressure. I was personally delighted how things had gone against Bestie. I'd face George in five semi-finals over all and we never let a goal in. The gaffer's tactics were spot on.

The whole occasion flashes past and it's over before you know it. Now there was the build to Leeds United's first visit to Wembley. At first you don't take in the enormity of reaching Wembley for the first time, it takes a while to sink in. Many of us were young, so you hope it will come around again and for a number of us it did. Often.

Our supporters were naturally euphoric and the race began for cup final tickets. The win over Manchester United was the first of many battles we had over the years with them and for our supporters it was and still is a massive game. For the players, Liverpool would be the big match over the coming decade, but for our fans, there is nothing like a clash against Manchester United.

By the time we faced Liverpool at Wembley, Manchester United had edged us to the title on goal average. A 1-0 defeat at Elland Road to United proving crucial in the end, nevertheless we had enjoyed a fantastic campaign in our first season back in the First Division.

There was no time to bemoan our luck as we had the FA Cup final against Liverpool ahead of us. At the time, only Alan Peacock and Johnny Giles had played at Wembley, so it was a new experience for the majority of us. The build up was great. We did a cup final song with Ronnie Hilton; there were some good singers and some awful singers amongst us!

For me, when I recall my first game at Wembley, it's not so much about who we played but the emotions of driving down Wembley Way and seeing the Twin Towers, it's absolutely amazing. You just want to get out onto the pitch. The dressing rooms for me were not that good, but it was Wembley. Then soaking up the atmosphere around the pitch before getting changed, lining up and walking up the tunnel and across the pitch. The weather was dreadful but that didn't matter. We lost, which was heartbreaking, but I knew we'd be back one day and win.

It was terribly disappointing to end up with nothing, and it would not be the first time, but how many teams would like to be in that position? Yes, it was a huge let down, but it was also a great achievement to get so close in our first season. Tottenham Hostpur achieved the double in 1960/61 to become the first team in the 21st century to do so to that point and only a few other teams had come close. We had joined that elite group and made a mark. As a club, we had become a force in the First Division and our day would come.

By the end of my career with Leeds United, I'd won numerous honours and achieved all my aims that I set out to do as a professional footballer. Winning the league titles was brilliant. As a one off, winning the FA Cup always sticks out. We lost more major honours than we actually won, but for a decade, we were always involved at the sharp end. The gaffer always played his strongest side, but playing in so many competitions there was fatigue towards the latter stages. It was not fear, it was fatigue and at crucial times, our form dipped, but I would not have it any other way because it was a brilliant time.

From a struggling Second Division outfit when I first came into the side we had come a long way. The 1964/65 campaign, although we came away with nothing, will always be memorable for me as it was our first crack at top-flight football and we certainly made our mark. By the end of the season, everyone knew about Leeds United. Our victory over Manchester United in the FA Cup semi-finals will always be particularly special. The elation afterwards was incredible. We were on our way as a team.

TERRY COOPER
LEFT-BACK 1961–1975

BORN   12th July 1944, Brotherton, Nr Pontefract
SIGNED   May 1961 as apprentice
LEEDS CAREER   351 games, 11 goals
HONOURS   1 Division One Championship, 1 League Cup, 2 Fairs Cups,
20 England caps
LEFT   Transferred to Middlesbrough, March 1975; £50,000

Terry was a swashbuckling attacking left-back, recognised as the finest
in his position at the 1970 World Cup finals in Mexico. Tactically astute,
a strong tackler and pinpoint crosser of the ball, Terry's pace enabled
him to link brilliantly with Eddie Gray on the left flank. Among 11
goals for Leeds, his most memorable claimed victory against Arsenal in
the League Cup final at Wembley in 1968, the club's first major honour.
A key member of the First Division title-winning team 12 months later,
Terry enhanced his reputation when Leeds won the Fairs Cup for a
second time, but a broken leg in April 1972 sidelined him for two years.

Arsenal 0 v Leeds United 1

League Cup Final
Saturday 2nd March 1968

Wembley Stadium
Attendance 97,887

Leeds United win their first major honour

Teams

Bertie Mee	**Managers**	Don Revie
Jim Furnell	1	Gary Sprake
Peter Storey	2	Paul Reaney
Bob McNab	3	Terry Cooper
Frank McLintock	4	Billy Bremner
Peter Simpson	5	Jack Charlton
Ian Ure	6	Norman Hunter
John Radford	7	Jimmy Greenhoff
David Jenkins	8	Peter Lorimer
(Sub. Terry Neill)		
George Graham	9	Paul Madeley
Jon Sammels	10	Johnny Giles
George Armstrong	11	Eddie Gray
		(Sub. Rod Belfitt)
	Scorers	Cooper 18

Referee: L Hamer

LEEDS UNITED had reached FA Cup and Fairs Cup finals and also finished as First Division runners-up when I broke into the side on a regular basis after converting from left-wing to left-back at the start of the 1967/68 campaign. We needed to win a trophy. The League Cup final that season will always be memorable because not only was it our first major honour, but I was in the right place to get our winning goal. The feeling afterwards was "that's the first." And that was right – it proved a springboard to further success.

I grew up in a little village called Brotherton, started the local school at five and left when I was 15. I wanted to be a footballer and always had a football with me. At school, there were only eight senior boys, so we could not play other schools regularly, but we did play twice a year against a local village team called Fairburn, which were big occasions.

I learned my football technique under the street lampposts. I'd come home from school, do my chores, gulp down my tea and play for hours pretending to be Stanley Matthews. I played football with my mates whenever possible. In the playground there were always games of cricket and girls skipping, plus me and my mates playing five-a-side football. I had to dodge people continually, which taught me to dribble, drop my shoulders and get a good first touch.

Everyone knew about Stanley Matthews. I read about him in Charles Buchan's Book of Football and the 1953 FA Cup final was the first I saw on television. The whole country was willing Matthews to get a Cup winner's medal. He inspired Blackpool to a famous victory and the match became known as the 'Matthews Final'. At the time I thought, "I'd love a go at that."

When I was about 13, I played football at the local Rec every Sunday. It was a bumpy pitch, but that didn't matter. Blokes would come along after the pubs closed. Taking them on while they tried to kick lumps out of you made me stronger, fitter and gave me an appreciation of how to beat opponents.

On Saturdays I began playing for Ferrybridge Amateurs. A Wolves scout invited me to play for Wolves' nursery team, Wath Wanderers, who played in the Northern Intermediate League. My first game was against Sunderland reserves and we lost 8-1. I touched the ball twice. Then we played Newcastle United, we lost 7-0. I didn't touch the ball. I thought I'd blown my chance, but I was asked to attend a trial at Molineux, which was a huge honour as Wanderers had been the biggest club of the 1950s. I scored, but it wasn't enough.

I returned home and played for Ferrybridge for three months when a Leeds United scout spotted me. Don Revie had been in charge two months and was looking for ground staff lads. I was determined to take my opportunity during a trial at Fullerton Park. I was working as an apprentice fitter on mining machinery at Fryston colliery, so my uncle picked me up. I arrived early with my boots wrapped in a newspaper, but I forgot my towel. Syd Owen loaned me one but gave me a rollicking. It was an early lesson.

I faced Paul Reaney, who was also trying to make an impression. Either Paul had an off day or let me play well because Don asked me to join the ground staff. I could not believe it. My mum was happy, but concerned I may be taking a risk as I had an apprenticeship earning £6 a week. I explained I'd be earning £20 a week. That was a fortune to mum. She said, "what if it goes wrong?" I said it could, but I might make it. That was all mum needed to hear. She said, "Terry, you've always wanted to be a footballer, give it a go."

I didn't sense anything special was developing. I certainly didn't think we'd all play international football, which was every young footballer's dream. I was just glad to be on the ground staff. We trained hard, had lunch, trained hard again then did duties that included painting barriers, weeding terracing and whitewashing the toilets.

Leeds United as a football club was struggling. As we made our way, the first team were bottom of the Second Division. Being 16, I thought they must be ordinary players. Not all were bad, though, because they had Freddie Goodwin, Ian Lawson and Jim Storrie. Jack Charlton was in the side, but a bit of a rebel and so was little Billy Bremner, who was precocious but talented.

Towards the end of the 1961/62 season, Don pulled off a masterstroke when he signed Bobby Collins, a top player at Celtic and Everton. Bobby's arrival brought a turnaround in Leeds fortunes as they stayed up against the odds. There was great relief, survival was crucial. Don believed the ground staff lads were the club's future, but knew the first team needed strengthening. His stroke of luck was that many apprentices who'd already joined the club would become first team regulars and internationals.

Bobby brought a winning mentality to the club and, although five foot nothing, fought like Goliath. Bobby was an amazing little man. Maybe at times he was a bit over the top, but Bobby led from the front and inspired all the younger players.

During the close season, I signed professional forms and near the end of the 1963/64 campaign, I made my first team debut as Leeds headed for promotion. Albert Johanesson was playing well, but when it came down to the nitty gritty, Don wanted solidity away from home. With just three games to go I played at Charlton Athletic in his place. If we won, we were up.

I was nervous, but I had Bobby inside me and from the first kick, he talked me through the game. "Come in here, go wide" and when someone touched me Bobby said, "forget it, leave that to me." In the next 10 minutes, bang, he'd flattened them and had a little word, "leave Terry alone." I thought, "what's he doing?" but Bobby was looking after me. Bobby was brilliant. For a young lad, watching at close hand how Bobby approached a game, how he prepared, his mental strength, it was superb.

Today, you hear people talk about coaching this and coaching that. As a young player, you learn more watching a top player than listening to 50 coaches. Bobby's example of talking me through my debut was something I tried to emulate later in my career when young players came through.

We defeated Charlton 3-0 to guarantee promotion back to the First Division. Although Albert returned for our final home game against Plymouth Argyle, I was back in the side for our trip to Swansea Town. We won 2-0 to tie up the title. My first two games were a baptism of fire. I loved every minute of them and wanted more.

The following season I got more opportunities, which was great, but I knew that I'd have to bide my time. During the campaign, I began to play left-back. Initially, it was Syd Owen who suggested to Don he should try me out in defence because, although I was a winger, I could tackle and got stuck in. During pre-season, Don pulled me aside and explained he was short when Willie picked an injury. I said I'd give it a go even though I'd never played in defence. Syd took me aside and guided me on positional play. I played left back in a few reserve games and, obviously, Syd told Don I had taken to it.

Early in the season, I had a three match run when Willie was injured. We lost at Blackpool, but defeated them in the return fixture and beat Leicester City. Willie returned, so I went back in the reserves, but I was pleased how things had gone. I had more chances of a run out as I could deputise in two positions. I came back into the side as we were battling alongside Manchester United at the top for our 1-0 win at Old Trafford. I also played in our run to the FA Cup final. We had tough away ties at Everton and Crystal Palace and that was when Don utilised me in midfield. Albert played at Hillsborough but picked up an injury so I came in for the replay at Nottingham Forest. I'd played in a few big games but this was something else. The atmosphere was electric. We came through with a last minute header from Billy. The scenes in our dressing room were fantastic.

I was in with a chance of playing at Wembley, but Don decided to play Albert. I wasn't upset at the time. I was delighted to be part of the squad and knew that if Albert did spark he could do a lot of damage. There were no substitutes, so I watched the game from the bench. Liverpool had a strong side; they had won the league a year earlier. We were underdogs and had chances to nick it, but lost 2-1. It was our first major final and in many ways; the occasion went over our heads, particularly the younger lads. It was a great experience, though, and gave us a thirst for more. Don later told me he made a mistake not playing me.

Over the next couple of seasons, I played in more high profile games, including the 1967 FA Cup semi-final against Chelsea. Our defeat to Chelsea was hard to take; I understood my two disallowed goals, but how Peter Lorimer's goal was ruled out was incredible. Peter leathered a free-kick and the ball flew in. I thought, "what's going on here?" People say the worst feeling is losing a semi-final. For me that's true. You are so near and it's every footballers dream to play in a showpiece final. It drains you. I did not want to speak to anyone. I just wanted to get on our team coach and go home. When you get done by a controversial decision it's so tough. If Chelsea had outplayed us, beaten us fair and square, you put your hands up and say "fair play," but losing like that you think, what's going on.

We were shell-shocked but Don, Syd Owen and Les Cocker were great at picking us up. They'd come round, talk to us individually, and say, come on we're still building the club, we've had a taster, forget about it. Have a good holiday, but when we come back for pre-season training we'll be there again challenging for honours.

I was happy at Leeds, but during the 1967/68 close season, I considered leaving. Don's only fault was that at times he was too loyal to players. Instead of saying, "this lad has come of age, you're in," I'd be dropped and it got frustrating. Without being derogatory to Albert, if we were playing a tough away game where the match would be physical, real muck and nettles stuff, then I'd play. Also, without being nasty to Willie Bell, I knew that I was a better player.

I spoke to senior players and they sympathised because they thought I should be in. They said, "ask for a transfer." Leicester City and Wolves were interested, so I put in a transfer request. Derek Dougan at Wolves and Davie Gibson at Leicester rang me to say I'd enjoy it at their clubs. I didn't want to leave, but felt that I had no choice. Luckily, before a fee was agreed, the boss put me into the side when Willie was injured a few games into the season.

It was a shame for Willie, but I had an opportunity and took it. Willie moved on. The feeling among the players was that it was just a question of when we'd win a major trophy, not if we'd win a trophy. Early on in the campaign, we had a chance when we faced Dynamo Zagreb in the delayed Fairs Cup final from the previous season, but it was not to be. After losing the first leg 2-0, we failed to break them down at Elland Road despite dominating possession.

It was a big disappointment, but honours would finally come our way because there was a lot of quality in our side. We had a solid defence. Gary Sprake could be sensational and stopped things he had no right to stop, but his lack of concentration sometimes resulted in a howler.

Early in the season, he threw the ball into his own goal at Anfield in front of the Kop. We couldn't believe it. Peter Thompson put a cross in and Gary caught it. I sprinted to the touchline and shouted "Sprakie," because Don liked me to move the ball forward quickly to get at opponents. On this occasion though, Gary saw Ian Callaghan closing in, changed his mind mid-throw and threw the ball into our goal. Big Jack sank to his knees on the penalty spot. The referee ran up to Jack and asked what happened; he was stunned when Jack told him.

Gary is often remembered for high profile mistakes, which is unfortunate because if I made a mistake, one of the lads could rescue me. If Gary made a mistake, there was generally nobody to rescue him. Gary was agile, had natural ability and was a great shot stopper. On many occasions, I believe, he saved us.

Paul Reaney was pound for pound the strongest player at the club. Wingers did not like playing against him, which I could understand because if you tried to push and run him, Paul was strong and quick. He could match anyone for pace. It was a good combination having Paul or myself at full-back. Paul being more defensive allowed me to get forward more.

Jack Charlton was probably the best centre-half England has produced, but you had to play with him to appreciate that because Jack looked ungainly. Big Jack was one of the quickest players at Leeds, five strides and he was at the halfway line. Jack had great ability for a tall chap and was a winner. He was also dangerous at set-pieces and scored a hatful of goals.

Norman Hunter was a fantastic player. I knew that if I went forward and got caught, Norman would cover me. He was a brilliant defender and had a fearsome reputation, wrongly really, because Norman had great ability and was not like that at all off the field. Norman could also bring the ball out from the back with ease. When we were really on top, Norman got a bit bored and wanted to be part of the passing movement. On many occasions, Les Cocker went berserk with Norman, Eddie and myself because I'd overlap Eddie, next thing Norman overlapped me. The balance down our left flank was incredible because not many teams could boast three naturally left-footed players.

Billy Bremner and Johnny Giles controlled midfield. They had teamed up when Bobby Collins suffered a terrible injury in Torino during our first Fairs Cup campaign. Billy was one of the best players I played with. He led by example. He didn't like training without a ball, if Billy trained with a ball, he would stop out 24 hours. Billy had the quickest feet that I have seen. Of course, he was also inspirational and if you needed a goal, Billy would pop up to score. He could score from close range, with headers or strike it home from long range. Billy was a tremendous footballer.

Johnny Giles was a different type of player to Billy. Johnny was more laid back, passed it off both feet, precision passing over 60 metres. Billy would get more into the box whereas Johnny would sit in there covering. Johnny could also look after himself, but as with us all, we had a good tutor in Bobby.

One area we struggled at times was in attack. We had not replaced Alan Peacock at centre-forward despite the best efforts of Peter Lorimer, Jimmy Greenhoff, Eddie Gray, Paul Madeley and Rod Belfitt. Don found the answer by signing Mick Jones from Sheffield United in September 1967. Peter would ultimately switch to the right wing, while Eddie replaced Albert on the left.

Jimmy Greenhoff was slim, had a mop of blond hair, lightening pace and great technique. He had everything to become a great player, and all the trimmings, but didn't fulfil his potential. Jimmy got frustrated because he was not playing regularly and moved on to Birmingham.

Peter Lorimer was renowned for his shooting ability. I remember Peter coming to the club at 15, pencil thin, and doing a shooting session with Syd Owen. Sprakie was in goal and we did one-twos. Peter did not appear to have a muscle in his thigh, but his shot was like a cannonball. His timing was perfect. Many of his goals were sensational, but for me Peter was underrated.

Eddie Gray was a throwback to the old Scottish winger. Eddie had everything. He was tall, powerful, had a great left peg, all the tricks. I ran off Eddie and we linked well together. Eddie would run the full-back infield and if the winger was tired and I had a yard on him, I'd go haring down the wing to put a cross in.

Paul Madeley never had a particular position, but always played. The previous season, Paul wore every outfield shirt except number 11. He was an invaluable team member and generally played in defence or midfield depending on tactics or if someone was injured.

Rod Belfitt was a player's player. He didn't have the best technique, but would go through a brick wall for you. Rod was a hard working striker. As for Mick Jones, who was cup-tied in the League Cup, all the lads still say that Mick was their favourite player. He was so unassuming, worked his socks off, was tremendous in the air and a great foil for other players.

We quickly began to challenge on four fronts. Don always wanted us to aim at everything and we certainly gave it our best shot. In the league we hammered Chelsea 7-0 and, come the New Year, we thumped Fulham and Southampton 5-0 in consecutive games.

In the cups, we made solid progress. I filled in on the left wing for our League Cup opening round victories against Luton Town and Bury. I was playing in the left-back position for our fifth round win at Sunderland before a comfortable victory over Stoke City. We drew Derby County in the semi-finals and came through 4-3 on aggregate over two legs. Reaching Wembley was so important to the players. There was real elation in the dressing room. We had a few drinks to celebrate that night. The boss was fine about it. Don used to say to Billy after a big win, "well done, make sure the lads have a good drink." He knew that we were responsible and would be up and running for the next match.

Getting to the final was great but we were determined to win this time. Our opponents were Arsenal, so it would be tough and they had fine players in the likes of Frank McLintock, Jon Sammels, John Radford and George Graham. The final took place mid-season, but unlike today, the game was not put back to a Sunday for live television. We played on the Saturday as usual, so had to reschedule another league fixture; highlights were shown the following day. We were fortunate though because a league game the week before was postponed due to the weather, so we had a two-week build up.

We stayed at Selsdon Park in Surrey, which was great. We had a bit of a loosener in terms of a training session with short, sharp exercises. We were playing so many games that the session was just a good warm up with a game of one-touch, two-touch 15-minute football. We were ready for the final and I was confident we would win.

Team spirit was terrific and that was down to the gaffer. He was an incredible person and always had a word for you. His man-management and attention to detail were his great strengths. We were a team of young lads and within a short space of time from not being many kiddies about the place there must have been 40. Every Christmas party, Don was Santa Claus and knew every kid's first name.

I remember moving into our first house in Garforth after getting married. It was a Wednesday. I went into the garden and ricked my back. There was no way I could train. Within an hour, the biggest basket of fruit you have ever seen arrived from the boss. A note said "Get well soon, I need you." When it arrived, I thought, "I can't stop in bed, the boss needs me." I was soon up because I wanted to play Saturday. If I went in and happened to say, 'my wife has flu,' a bouquet of flowers would arrive at home within an hour. That was the boss.

We had a squad, but if it was possible to play, we all did, even with injuries. Les would strap you up. I remember playing with a broken toe for around six weeks. I didn't train during the week. Thirty minutes before kick off, the Doc would give me a pain-killing injection. For 75 minutes, I'd be fine but the last 15 minutes my toe would be excruciating and would be swollen afterwards. We all did it, though, because we did not want to let the boss and our team-mates down. If it was at all possible to play, we did.

This was my first visit to Wembley since seeing Leeds in the '65 cup final. To go back as a player was tremendous. It's the mystique of the stadium that is fantastic. The League Cup final had been moved to Wembley a year earlier giving it more prestige. Going down Wembley Way was great and then walking around the pitch, I thought, "Wembley is in good nick today."

The main thing that hit me was when we came out of the tunnel. The Leeds supporters were at that end. The noise was deafening. I knew from the lads that played in '65 that the noise would hit me, but until you actually walk out at Wembley, you do not know what to expect. It was quite a long tunnel that you walk down. You're walking and talking and you cannot hear anything. Then, Bang, it hits you. Then you meet the dignitaries and when they play the national anthem, it is moving. I thought, "this isn't bad."

From the start, there was an edge to the game as both sides settled. Tackles were flying in. After 18 minutes, I opened the scoring and it's a goal I'll never forget. When we got a corner, as usual I moved up to the edge of the box to keep the pressure up in case anything came out. I remember the ball coming over from Eddie Gray's corner kick. Big Jack and Paul Madeley went up with Arsenal keeper Jim Furnell. The ball fell to Ian Ure who headed it out.

I was loitering 20 yards from goal when the ball dropped nicely just inside the penalty box, I thought, "close your eyes and leather it," which I did. When I opened my eyes, I could see the ball flying into the top corner of the net. My goal was in some ways a fluke, because my shot flew in, but it could just as easily have hit someone in the crowd or knocked over the corner flag. Arsenal complained bitterly that Big Jack and Paul had blocked Furnell, but the goal stood.

During the build up in the week of the final, a story had gone round that I'd dreamt about scoring the winning goal. That was true, but it was taken out of all proportion, as I'm sure other players did too. All these years on, I still dream I'm playing for Leeds United, wearing the sock tabs and white shirt with Norman, Big Jack and the lads, but then I wake up and think, "silly bugger!"

My strike angered the Arsenal players and the match became a bitter tussle. There were lots of fouls, niggling incidents and stoppages in play. Any late challenge brought a reaction from both sides and there were a couple of ugly incidents when players jostled each other. The worst occurred just before half-time when Frank McLintock fouled Gary Sprake and Ian Ure rushed in late. We were not impressed and let the Arsenal players know. It took the referee some time to calm things down.

During the break, Don felt another opportunity would come, but if it didn't we had to keep it tight. We were so determined because we had fallen at the final hurdle a number of times. Jogging back out only 45 minutes separated us from our first major trophy.

With Billy covering every blade of grass and Johnny Giles controlling things in the middle, we had a tight stranglehold on the game, but we had to keep concentrating throughout. As an attacking force, we battled away with little joy, although we felt aggrieved when the referee turned down our penalty appeals near the end when Furnell seemed to impede Big Jack.

Arsenal didn't really trouble us at all in the second half. Norman was quick to break up any attacks down the middle, Big Jack was dominant in the air while Paul and myself was not letting anything past us. Sprakie had little to do throughout the match apart from take crosses although he did have a scare 20 minutes from time when Peter Simpson appealed for a penalty after a clash between the two, but the referee was not impressed. Gary was also on hand to push a John Radford effort around the post as Arsenal tried to throw everything at us.

Overall, defences dominated and it made for a dour game. For the neutral fan, there was little to cheer, with few clear-cut chances. We had a goal lead and were determined to hold on. The result was all-important. We had to win that trophy.

At the final whistle, there was great elation. I remember Norman shaking his fist, "that's the first one." Everyone was hugging and it was great walking up those famous Wembley steps to receive our tankards before showing the League Cup to the supporters. Back in the dressing room, there was relief and a feeling that it was a job well done. We were happy and had a good night at the Savoy. We had the trophy there and enjoyed a sing-along at the piano.

On the Sunday, I remember coming back on the train with the League Cup. The atmosphere was fantastic in the city as we had a parade to Leeds Town Hall before a civic reception. Thousands turned out, which was terrific, but the timing could have been better as the highlights of the final were on ITV at the same time – and of course in that day and age the game had not been on live! In 1968, video recorders were not a common household product, so they all missed seeing the match, but they saw us bring home the trophy.

The media criticised us for being too defensive, but Arsenal didn't come out with much credit either. For everyone connected with Leeds United, victory was what mattered after a number of disappointments. We had claimed our first major honour. All these years later, it's great to be associated with it because of my goal.

I scored 11 for Leeds in my career. I remember three. The one against Arsenal at Wembley, a right footer against Chelsea when we won 5-2 at Stamford Bridge in January 1970 and one that 'screamed' in against Newcastle United on Boxing Day 1966. I was not supposed to play against Newcastle because I had an upset stomach, but Albert went down overnight. When I got to the ground, the boss said I was playing. I said, "oh no!" but I did and scored. I remember Big Jack giving me a rollicking during the game. He yelled, "Hey, Terry, why don't you start moving your arse." "Okay Jack,: I replied I remember the ball coming towards me. I got my head down, made a yard and hit it. The ball bobbled across the keeper and trickled in the corner. I went over to Jack and gave him some stick.

Winning the League Cup was tremendous and we felt, "right, that's one under our belt now let's win the championship, FA Cup and Fairs Cup." In other words all the other trophies! We missed out in the FA Cup to Everton at the semi-final stage a month after winning the League Cup, which was hugely disappointing and eventually finished fourth in the league. In the Fairs Cup we made it all the way to the final where we played Ferencvaros, which was held over to the start of the next season. The Hungarian side had the boy Florian Albert playing, who had fantastic skill. In the second leg, Gary Sprake was superb and we held onto a 1-0 first leg lead to claim our first European trophy.

By the end the 1968/69 campaign, we'd clinched the championship following a 0-0 draw at Liverpool. That was some atmosphere. Everyone remembers that game because the lads went to the Anfield Kop and received fantastic acclaim from the Liverpool supporters. I missed out on that moment because I'd already walked off. I was near the player's tunnel when the final whistle went, so jogged off for a shower, but soon wondered where everyone else was. The lads came in and asked where I'd been because the Kop had been singing to them. I thought, "missed it again Terry," typical me.

Of course, we went on to more success and it was a fantastic time to play for Leeds United. We grew up together. If someone kicked me there were 10 lads looking after me. I was fortunate to be part of something very special. The camaraderie was tremendous; the trophies were a bonus and, of course, it all started with that victory over Arsenal at Wembley. That meant so much to everyone connected with Leeds United and I'm proud to have played my part in it.

NORMAN HUNTER
CENTRE-HALF 1962–1976

BORN   24th October 1943, Eighton Banks, County Durham
SIGNED   November 1960 as apprentice
LEEDS CAREER   726 games, 21 goals
HONOURS   2 Division One Championships, 1 Division Two Championship,
1 FA Cup, 1 League Cup, 2 Fairs Cups, 28 England caps, 3 England U23 caps
LEFT   Transferred to Bristol City, October 1976

Norman was renowned as one of the classic 'hard' men alongside Ron
Harris, Dave Mackay and Tommy Smith. A ferocious tackler, Norman
was the only player in Don Revie's legendary squad to appear in every
major cup final. Player of the Year in 1971 and PFA Player of the Year
in 1973, Norman was quick, committed and possessed great positional
awareness, He could also play his way out of defence, support the attack
and packed a thunderous shot, scoring 21 goals. Norman 'Bites yer
Legs' Hunter played more European ties than any other Leeds player
(78) and is one of five players to make over 700 appearances for the club.

Ferencvaros 0 v Leeds United 0

Fairs Cup Final second leg
Wednesday 11th September 1968

Nep Stadium, Budapest
Attendance 76,000

Leeds United win their first European trophy

Teams

Károly Lakat	**Managers**	Don Revie
Istvan Geczi	1	Gary Sprake
Dezso Novak	2	Paul Reaney
Miklos Pancsics	3	Terry Cooper
Sandor Havasi	4	Billy Bremner
Istvan Juhasz	5	Jack Charlton
Lajos Szucs	6	Norman Hunter
Istvan Szoke	7	Mike O'Grady
(Sub. Janes Karaba)		
Zoltan Varga	8	Peter Lorimer
Florian Albert	9	Mick Jones
Gyula Rakosi	10	Paul Madeley
Sandor Katona	11	Terry Hibbitt
		(Sub. Mick Bates)

Scorers

Referee: G Schulenberg

THE FAIRS CUP was a hard competition and there were plenty of crack outfits taking part every season. I loved a midweek game under the floodlights, despite facing opposition we had never played against and players we had not heard of or seen play because there was little television footage. I psyched myself up for European games. All right, you got your blood twisted sometimes by the technical types with balls flicked in and one-twos around the box. You had to be on your mettle more than in domestic football. Opponents did something unusual, but they did not like the physical contact. The game was also more on the floor than in the air. We had some tremendous battles over the years and won the trophy twice. So to win the trophy against Ferencvaros, a crack Hungarian side in 1968, meant we had arrived as a force in Europe.

From an early age, I was into sports, especially football. My family was Newcastle United through and through. The area where we lived was steeped in football. At school, our teacher would ask us what we hoped to do. I replied, "I'm going to play football." My classmates laughed, but I wasn't joking. Playing football was what I wanted to do. My hero was Jackie Milburn. I watched Newcastle on television when they played in three FA Cup finals in the 50s, defeating Blackpool, Arsenal and Manchester City. They had a great cup tradition.

I didn't like going to games because of the packed crowds. Even today, I'm not that comfortable watching matches with massive crowds around me. At St. James's Park, if you arrived late, fans would pass you down over their heads and shout, "boy coming down". I'd tie my money and bits in my handkerchief, stuff it in my pocket and hang on while I was lowered down to the front of the stand. It was unnerving.

I would have crawled on my hands and knees to play for Newcastle United, but they did not come in for me. I made progress and got into the district side, but not the county team because I was not physically big enough. I played for Birtley Secondary Modern School, Birtley Juniors and Chester-le-Street. Eventually, a Leeds United scout asked me to a trial. I played against Bradford Park Avenue and we won by six. Shortly after, I was asked to join the ground staff.

When I arrived at Elland Road, the manager was Jack Taylor. Don Revie was coming to the end of his playing career. I lived in digs in Beeston along with little Billy [Bremner]. At first, I was a bit homesick and could not wait to get home, but soon got into the swing of things.

I was not as talented as some apprentices were at Leeds, but at 17, Jack Taylor kept me on. Why, I don't know, but he told me, "Norman, you're not big enough or strong enough but we'll give you six months." During the six months, Jack got the sack. I was not surprised, because there was no respect for him. At one team meeting, players were throwing streamers around the room and then during circuit training, some lads threw equipment down the banking. It was out of order, but strong discipline was lacking. The club was in turmoil if I'm honest. I could tell that and I was a young apprentice.

When Don Revie became manager in March 1961, Leeds United was very different to what it became. Leeds Rugby League Club got bigger crowds [Leeds gate for the home game against Luton was under 10,000], but with Don in charge, suddenly the youngsters were given a chance. It was phenomenal. Of course, plenty of lads didn't make it, but the number that had top flight careers was amazing. The talent Leeds United attracted became the backbone of Don's great side for the next 15 years.

My move from inside-left to defence came about when the gaffer asked striker Jim Storrie which kids were good when he played against them. Jim, so the story goes, told the gaffer, "Every time that Norman Hunter goes back, he gets a touch, tackles me or takes the ball off me. He doesn't look as if he knows what he is doing, but he does."

The gaffer asked me to play in defence against Manchester United reserves. I must have done OK, because six games into the 1962/63 season, Don gave me my first team debut against Swansea Town. After the previous season's struggle against relegation, Don decided it was time for change. It was a risk as we were so inexperienced, but he knew he had promising youngsters. Now he felt was the time to blood a few and I was one of four, alongside Gary Sprake, Paul Reaney, Rod Johnson. I replaced Freddie Goodwin. We came away with a 2-0 win. We remained in the side and finished the season fifth, which was a massive improvement. I even scored a couple of goals, the second giving us a win at Charlton Athletic. Leeds' other scorer was my partner in central defence, Jack Charlton.

The club was going forward. Bobby Collins was the inspiration. Bobby's character and personality was stamped on the team early doors.

This little fellow, five foot four inches of grit, would yell at us, "Come on; get stuck in". He'd turn to me and demand, "Norm, show them that way", then in would come this little fellow, bang! He wasn't only a tough tackler, though. Bobby was a great passer, could hit a ball and bend it. He was one of the first players I saw perfect the 'banana' shot. What a great player. Bobby above everyone set the standards at Leeds United.

In 1963/64, promotion was the target. The gaffer strengthened the side by bringing in Johnny Giles and, towards the run-in, centre-forward Alan Peacock. It was a battle, but we only lost once after the turn of the New Year and clinched promotion with a professional display at Swansea to win 3-0. In our final game, we secured the title with a 2-0 win at Charlton. Alan scored twice in both matches.

Pundits tipped us to go down from the First Division in 1964/65, but they couldn't have been more wrong. In fact, the gaffer was great at turning what people said about us around to our advantage. Looking back, with the characters and personalities we had, there was no way on this earth we were going down. We would not have let it happen. Instead we had a great season. How many teams are promoted then come within goal average of winning the league and lose out in the FA Cup final in extra-time? At the time, it was heartbreaking, but when we came back pre-season, we knew that this team was going places and of course, we'd also be playing in the Fairs Cup for the first time.

During our first European campaign, we overcame the loss of Bobby Collins following a horrendous challenge by one of their players, to beat Torino. After beating Leipzig, we faced Valencia. It was a bad-tempered clash. In the first leg at Elland Road, three players were sent off, including Big Jack. Whenever we got a set piece, Jack would go and stand on their goal line. He was not doing anything wrong, but late on, Valencia's keeper had obviously had enough and punched him. Next thing I know he is running behind the goal with Jack chasing him. Jack landed some blows and then police had to separate fighting players before both sides were sent to cool down in the dressing rooms. We drew 1-1. In the return, we snatched a brilliant win with a Mike O'Grady goal.

It was far more comfortable against Hungarians Ujpest Dozsa, we used to call them 'upsadaisy', before we faced Real Zaragoza in the semi-finals. During our run, the gaffer tried all sorts of tactics. We wore different numbers to normal in one game, then we watered the pitch before our semi-final play-off against Zaragoza [the tie finished 2-2 after the first two legs and the modern away goals rule did not operate at that time], but after 20 minutes, they led 3-0. Zaragoza was a good team and it was a disappointing way to end our run, but we'd gained tremendous experience.

The following season, after qualifying again by finishing second in the league once again, we comfortably defeated DWS Amsterdam 8-2 on aggregate, had another tough battle with Valencia before beating Bologna on the toss of a disc when their captain chose incorrectly after we'd drawn 1-1 on aggregate. In the semi-finals, a Rod Belfitt hat-trick in the first leg was enough to see us through 4-2 against Kilmarnock to our first European final against the top Yugoslavian side Dynamo Zagreb, but they beat us 2-0 at their place and held onto a 0-0 draw at Elland Road.

It was a big disappointment again, but reaching a semi-final and final in our opening two campaigns was some going. We liked playing in Europe, but some of the travelling was unbelievable. Buses, trains and planes; at times, it took forever. Then there was an important league game. It was a problem, especially when we were going for a number of trophies at the same time.

At the start of the 1967/68 campaign, we really wanted to register our first 'major' honour. We were confident it would come; it was only a matter of time. Since promotion we'd finished as First Division runners-up twice, reached an FA Cup semi-final and final; and also gone close in Europe on two occasions. By then only Tottenham Hotspur and Celtic of Britain's clubs had won a European trophy. We wanted to join them.

By early New Year we were challenging on four fronts. Winning the League Cup final against Arsenal was a big win for the club. It was lift off for us. Our confidence was sky high, but the games began to stack up and we went out of the FA Cup to Everton in the semi-finals and fell away in the league, but our consistency in Europe took us to a third final in four years.

Our passage was comfortable. After a club record 16-0 win over amateur side Spora Luxembourg, draws away from home against Partizan Belgrade and Hibernian took us through. It was tight against Hibernian and we only booked a quarter-final clash against Rangers with a goal by Big Jack late on in the second leg to earn a 2-1 aggregate victory.

There was so much demand by Leeds fans for first leg tickets in Glasgow; the match was beamed back to Elland Road where over 20,000 watched on a giant screen. The atmosphere at Ibrox when we faced Rangers was electric, but our away form earned a hard-fought 0-0 draw before goals by Gilesy, and Peter Lorimer set up a semi-final with Dundee.

By the time we faced Dundee we'd already played 59 matches that season, many more than other clubs. We were jaded, but dug deep. Paul Madeley earned us a 1-1 draw at Easter Road, before Eddie Gray sealed another 2-1 aggregate victory in front of our home fans packed into three stands due to structural work on the Spion Kop roof.

We fancied our chances, but the final would not take place until the start of our 1968/69 campaign. Our opponents were crack Hungarian side Ferencvaros, winners of the Fairs Cup in 1965. Ferencvaros had beaten Liverpool during this competition, not to mention our old friends Zaragoza, and overcame Bologna in the semi-finals. The Hungarians had a terrific forward line in Istvan Szoke, Zoltan Varga, Florian Albert, Gyula Rakosi and Sandor Katona. They were quick, skilful and balanced.

Ferencvaros would cause problems, but our style of play suited the European game. We had a balanced defence with natural lefties and rights. We didn't play flat at the back. If TC [Terry Cooper] was being attacked, I'd move along with Big Jack and Paul [Reaney]. I knew that I could attack the ball because instinctively there would be cover behind me.

We didn't tactically talk about defending deep. It just happened. If we went one up away from home, instead of getting another and another to make the game easy, we sat back while opponents came at us. We kept it tight and hit them on the break with the likes of Peter Lorimer, Billy Bremner, Shady [Mike] O'Grady and Eddie Gray. If we got a chance, nine times out of 10, these lads would bury it.

Ferencvaros were maybe more technical individually, but we were more together as a team. I enjoyed facing a technical player; it was a challenge. I had to get close to my opponent, close him down, see what he had under his shirt and how brave he was. If he skinned me then fair enough. Not everything can go your way on a football field. You can't always walk on and dominate somebody, you're going to come across someone quicker, someone that puts the ball through your legs, but that was the beauty of playing opposition you had never played before.

I was confident and felt we would win as we had a tremendous team spirit. Billy and Gilesy were characters in the dressing room. It was always those two if anything was flying around. We got in and took the Mickey out of each other. Training was never hard apart from a Tuesday if there was no midweek game, which was rare. Five-a-sides were fierce, the banter was terrific and the first team squad strong.

The big man [Jack Charlton] was kingpin. We fitted in around him; actually, he told us what to do nine times out of 10. Big Jack was like a traffic warden. He'd point to us, "Norm go here, Paul go there, pick him up Gilesy." He'd have us running all over the place, but, when it came to attacking the ball, he was the best centre-half I played with. What people don't realise is that he could fly. Anything chucked over the top I was not worried one iota. When there was not a lot at stake, the big man could be a bit sloppy and would tell everyone else off, but if it was an important game or if somebody annoyed him, Jack was superb.

Labels stick and my reputation preceded me. It wasn't that I was a harder tackler than the big man, TC or Paul Reaney, but I did go in a bit wild sometimes. In my era, everyone knew that the first tackle you made was to let a forward know you were there. If they stayed down, I had an easy afternoon. If they jumped up, I had a game on my hands. Later in my career, a banner saying 'Norman Bites Yer Legs' appeared at Elland Road and that stuck after it was seen on TV and reported in the papers. There's even a radio company called 'Bites Yer Legs' these days! I'm not complaining, because people do remember me. It's nice in a way, but compared to some players I was not hard. I saw danger coming; hard players didn't. Willie Bell was hard; he would dive in headfirst when boots were flying about. I'd think, "Willie, what are you doing?"

I had a reputation, but I could also play a bit, although I did not often get the opportunity. It did annoy me at times, but with the players Leeds had in front of me, I had no alternative. Billy and Gilesy always found space and demanded the ball. I could not win. If I passed the ball to the Irishman (Gilesy), the Scotsman (Billy) told me off and if I passed it to the Scotsman then the Irishman told me off. It was mostly Gilesy, though, and, after winning the ball, I'd hear, "yes, Norm". They were not the only choices, though, as I had TC, Eddie on the left, Paul and Peter on the right. I was spoiled for choice.

Billy Bremner never knew when he was beaten. Billy could play; he'd get on the ball and come up with the goods. Billy was not the greatest trainer, unless there was a football at his feet, but he had this drive. For Billy, it was a game of football, it was Leeds United and he was going to win. He'd teamed up with Johnny Giles in central midfield and they were tremendous as a partnership. It was some task taking over from Bobby Collins, but Gilsey was up to it. He distributed the ball superbly; he had a terrific strike and could look after himself.

Eddie Gray had amazing skills. I'd give it to Eddie, "here you go pal, take them on," and he did. Eddie was unfortunate with the injuries he picked up, but, when fit, there was no-one more skilful. One of the reasons Don was able to play the same side week-in week-out was because he had Paul Madeley. No matter who got injured, bar the goalkeeper, Paul came in. It was in some ways detrimental to Paul because his best position was alongside the centre-half at right-back, but that was Paul Reaney's place. What a great player, though, Madeley's versatility was amazing.

Peter Lorimer was one of the most underrated players we had, but even in training Peter was a great player. When you look at the goals he scored as a right-winger, it was phenomenal and his number of assists was also unbelievable. Peter was not the best at getting past people, but with his short back lift he could deliver it. Peter was one of the best strikers of a football I have seen.

From when I came into the side, a number of strikers had led the line, but none could match Mick Jones. Jonah came in and I've always said, if he'd had Allan Clarke's belief, then he would have been out of this world. Great player as Mick was, he didn't truly believe in himself. Mick had the ability, as all top centre-forwards have, to get off the floor and hang. Mick caused problems for opponents.

Although the gaffer knew his first choice team and played it whenever possible, we also had good squad players. Mick Bates could have got into most top sides, but was happy to deputise for one of the midfield players. It's funny how things fall for you. Mick was playing out of his skin at one stage when Gilesy regained fitness. The gaffer had a big decision to make, but then Mick picked up an injury. Don probably would have gone for Johnny, but Mick was a good player, no doubt about it.

Terry Hibbitt also came in at times and what a great left foot he had. Terry struggled to get a first team place, but when he went to Newcastle United, Malcolm Macdonald told me that he loved playing with him because, when he set off, he knew the ball would arrive just in front of him. Terry was a good player, but he was never going to get into our team regularly. Mike O'Grady had three years when he was playing well, but never really recovered from a troublesome back injury. When fit, though, Mike was dangerous on the right wing, as he gave us pace and had a great shot.

The home leg of the final was played on August Bank Holiday, which affected the attendance. Some supporters stayed away because it was shown live on BBC, the first televised game at Elland Road. It was very disappointing, especially with the Kop open again. As Ferencvaros wore all white, we changed our strip to blue tops and yellow shorts.

Ferencvaros came to defend and did so ruthlessly. There was persistent body checking and shirt pulling. They came looking for a draw and packed nine players back at the slightest hint of danger. The match was dour and contained far too many fouls to allow flowing football. We had a full strength team out, but could not break through a resolute defence. We could have gone a goal behind early on when Szoke blazed wide after being set up by Albert following a mistake Big Jack. Minutes later, Peter Lorimer should have opened the scoring when Mick Jones set him up from a free kick, but Ferencvaros keeper Geczi saved Peter's effort.

Szoke went close again, which was an escape for us but we made them pay from a corner kick just before half-time. Peter curled in a dangerous corner, Jack headed the ball down and Mick was on hand to force the ball home. As in the League Cup final when Arsenal felt their keeper had been fouled by Jack, so too did Ferencvaros, but as at Wembley, the goal stood.

Ferencvaros became even more defensive in the second half, but were still dangerous on the break, so we had to be on our mettle. Szoke almost grabbed an equaliser when Albert broke through, then Sprakie pulled off a brilliant stop to deny Rakosi. We lost Gilesy due to him having double vision and Mick Jones following heavy challenges, but we stayed firm.

The second half included a number of rash challenges. Both managers complained about each other's tactics afterwards, which added spice to the second leg at the Nep Stadium in Budapest. In the build up to the return, Ferencvaros boasted that our one goal lead would not be enough, but we had only ever let in more than one goal once in Europe away from home. We knew how to defend and soak up pressure. With Johnny Giles and Eddie Gray injured, the gaffer brought in Terry Hibbitt and Mike O'Grady.

From the kick-off, Ferencvaros were a different side to the one we faced at Elland Road. They were more attack-minded and we had to soak up enormous pressure. They came at us through the middle, down the flanks, on the ground and in the air. It was our most searching test to date in Europe, but we were up to the task. Big Jack won everything in up top, while Paul, TC and myself tackled anyone coming at us. We had to be disciplined and refused to be intimidated by a passionate 76,000 crowd. We had ten men behind the ball at times, leaving Mick as the lone striker. The tactics worked as we kept Fenecvaros at bay in the opening 15 minutes, before we had a break when TC acrobatically cleared a Rakosi shot off our goal line with an overhead kick. He then diverted an Albert shot wide. Sprakie also was in inspired form, pulling off a sensational save with a one-handed punch from a fierce free-kick by Ferencvaros captain Novak.

We had to play on the break and almost scored a crucial away goal on 30 minutes when Mick headed a Mike O'Grady cross onto the crossbar. Mike himself went close with a shot that caught Geczi by surprise, but we were soon defending again and were well satisfied to get into the dressing room with our first leg lead intact. The gaffer told us to keep things tight and felt confident we would come out winners. He had a word of encouragement for us all.

On the resumption, Sprakie was in inspired form, saving brilliantly from Szoke. The pattern of play was clear; we would be defending for long periods. Rakosi was just wide with an effort from a Varga cross, but we were holding firm. Just past the hour, Don strengthened midfield by replacing the more creative Terry Hibbitt with Mick Bates.

I loved those kind of games where we had plenty to do at the back and were under heavy pressure. I lapped up the work we had to get through and enjoyed the challenge, both mental and physical.

With the minutes ticking by, our bench kept us informed how long remained. We were very close to a famous triumph. Varga almost put a team-mate in with a clever overhead kick and in the final moments Albert had one last mazy run, but could not breach our defence. It had been a magnificent rearguard action. All the defence played well and Sprakie was outstanding. He had one of those nights when nothing was going to get past him. Everyone knows about the games in which Gary made a mistake, but against Fenercvaros he was awesome.

At the final whistle, there was a great relief. We had done it. Sir Stanley Rous, President of the Fairs Cup Committee, presented Billy with the trophy. We had a civic reception back in Leeds, but it took some time to take in what we had achieved. We received praise from all the British newspapers and had made ourselves a force at home and in Europe. Local journalist Phil Brown under the headline 'United's finest hour' summed up our display as one-for-all and all-for-one. That was us all over.

Winning the Fairs Cup was a great achievement and we went on to reach five finals in Europe, which was a tremendous accomplishment and something very few English sides have managed. We had some great battles. Certain opponents played man for man, and technically many countries were on a par if not ahead of us, but when it came to being cynical, no team could match Napoli. We played them during our defence of the trophy first time around. We won the first leg at home 2-0 when Big Jack nodded two in, but they pulled it back to 2-2 in the return. Late on was the only time I was frightened on a football field. They kicked us, spat at us, punched us and fell down on the floor at the slightest touch. There were bottles raining down.

Towards the end, their winger flung himself at Paul Madeley causing a bad gash on his thigh. The gaffer was really upset and before extra time said, "lads, I don't care what this result is, go out there and sort them out." This was the only time the gaffer ever said this. Big Jack was the first one to go in – whack. All of a sudden, everyone piled in. Napoli did not know what had hit them. People who were being 'brave', when it boiled down to the fight, were not so brave. It was war, absolute war. To cap it all little Billy won the toss of a coin to send us through. We were on the coach floor when we came out of the ground going up a steep ramp with bricks and bottles being thrown at us.

Our win over Juventus in 1971 was tremendous, but we suffered misery in the Cup Winners' Cup final two years later when the referee was banned for life and our European adventure ended when we lost the European Cup final. It was a night decisions went against us, especially when Beckenbaur kicked Clarkie up in the air for what looked a certain penalty and then Peter had a goal harshly chalked off. Losing to Bayern was one of the lowest points of my career, although coming from the North-East, the true lowest point was losing to Sunderland in the 1973 FA Cup final.

For all the lows, there were also many highs and winning a trophy abroad was a magical experience. We were not favourites, Ferencvaros had openly fancied their chances, but we put in one of our greatest ever away displays that night.

The gaffer was the main man and you never questioned his decisions out loud, but at times, I think he was too cautious. He could have let the reigns go a little bit, but he was the man, he was the boss and was different class. At times we played tremendous football. Everyone remembers when we hit seven against Southampton and five against Manchester United in 1972, but there were many other top class performances.

The only time I defied the gaffer was with being called up to play for England. He used to say, "Norman, you won't play, so don't go" but I insisted. Don was only concerned about Leeds United, which was fair comment and it's no different to the modern game when players are pulled out of squads. I would do anything for the gaffer, but I was part of the England squad and felt it was right to go.

People have often asked me, if it was frustrating not playing because Bobby Moore was first choice. When I was young and wanted to be in the team, I wanted to get in there. However, I sat and watched this magnificent fellow. Bobby was slower than I was, he wasn't great in the air, but his reading of the game, technical ability and first touch were awesome.

Bobby could pass like a midfielder. He'd pick it up and knock it in to Geoff Hurst, Roger Hunt or Jimmy Greaves. I watched a re-run of the 1966 World Cup final recently and Bobby was awesome, but didn't get a mention because what he did was simply expected. The better the opposition, the better Bobby played. I was better at club level than Bobby was; it suited my game. I liked the hustle and bustle, whereas with England it was more technical. Bobby was better at international level.

Looking back, maybe Leeds got involved in the latter stages of too many competitions, but the gaffer wanted to play the same team week in and week out, which meant we all played with injuries at times. One incident, I'll never forget. I'd had a kick on the ankles. Both were swollen. It was a Friday morning; I'd had treatment and was going to the ground for a fitness test. The missus said, "You have to be crackers," but I went down anyway. The gaffer asked how I felt and I told him that I was struggling, but as usual, he said, "Look I'd rather have a three-quarter fit you playing than anyone else." Well, all of a sudden, I felt OK. He never failed to convince you.

Most teams would get to a final and savour the build up. We didn't have time because there were still games to play and it took its toll. In 1967/68, we fell away and in 1969/70, we missed everything. The disappointments were great, but we always bounced back. We had a good set of lads. All right, we did not win as much as we should have done. I played in 10 finals and won four. Seven would have been a better ratio, but we did win four. Outside Yorkshire, we didn't go down as one of the great teams, but we were one of the best this country has ever produced. The players we faced recognise that. We could play and we could mix it. I remember teams coming to Elland Road and laying down before they stepped out, that's how dominant we were.

For me it was all about the spirit, the togetherness. It was unbelievable over a long period. I played over 700 games for Leeds, the majority with the Billys, the Jacks, the Peters and the Eddies. When I think about Leeds United now, for me it's about the lads from the mid-60s through to the early-70s and what we did together. It was about the boss at the helm, of course, and Billy as skipper too. But all the lads were in it together. I could not have wished for a better career. I used to wake up every morning and want to go down to that ground. It was magic.

JOHNNY GILES
MIDFIELD 1963–1975

BORN   6th January 1940, Dublin
SIGNED   August 1963 from Manchester United; £33,000
LEEDS CAREER   527 games, 115 goals
HONOURS   2 Division One Championships, 1 Division Two
Championship, 1 FA Cup, 1 League Cup, 2 Fairs Cups, 59 Ireland caps
LEFT   Transferred to West Bromich Albion, June 1975

Johnny was one of the great midfield generals of his generation. Possessing exceptional passing ability, he was a master tactician, scored his share of goals and could mix it when it got physical. In tandem with Billy Bremner, Johnny orchestrated proceedings from the centre of the park for Revie's great team. A sublime striker of the ball over any distance, Johnny hit double figures on five occasions during a season. Top scorer in 1966/67 with 18 goals, among his overall tally this skilful Irishman scored 44 penalties, the most by a Leeds United player.

Liverpool 0 v Leeds United 0

League Division One
Monday 28th April 1969

Anfield
Attendance 53,750

Leeds United clinch the First Division championship for the first time in their history

Teams

Bill Shankly	Managers	Don Revie
Tommy Lawrence	1	Gary Sprake
Chris Lawler	2	Paul Reaney
Geoff Strong	3	Terry Cooper
Tommy Smith	4	Billy Bremner
Ron Yeats	5	Jack Charlton
Emlyn Hughes	6	Norman Hunter
Ian Callaghan	7	Mike O'Grady
Bobby Graham	8	Paul Madeley
Alun Evans	9	Mick Jones
Ian St John	10	Johnny Giles
Peter Thompson	11	Eddie Gray

Scorers

Referee: A Dimond

I WAS FORTUNATE TO win numerous honours during my career, but anything you win for the first time is a special memory, because it is a breakthrough. Winning something again is a great thrill. Most players, if they are lucky, remember the first game, first international, first cup final and, if you are fortunate, a first league title. Our Championship triumph in 1968/69 was particularly special. The night we clinched it at Anfield against our great rivals Liverpool may not have been a classic match, but the achievement, knowing we were the best, was a special experience.

I'd wanted to be a footballer for as long as I can remember. From when I was a kid I was kicking a ball. Although I played a bit of Gaelic football in school, I loved football, without knowing anything about the game, because I could improvise. Manchester United was our team as kids because their captain Johnny Carey was a great Irish international player.

By the time I was 14, I'd played for a number of teams including Brunswick Street School, Dublin and Republic of Ireland Schools, Dublin City FC, The Leprechauns and Home Farm. While playing for Home Farm, a Manchester United scout spotted me. I arrived at the club in 1957 when the Busby Babes were the outstanding team in English football. They had a young side packed with talent and won the league twice before the Munich air disaster. I used to say "hello" to the players; it was a terrible tragedy.

I made my first team debut at the start of the 1959/60 season and played regularly until the end to the 1962/63 campaign when we won the FA Cup. After the Cup final, I played in the Charity Shield when we lost to Everton 4-0. Matt Busby left me out of the team after our defeat. I asked Matt for a transfer and he agreed to let me go. Don Revie came in for me and I signed for Leeds United straight away.

When you move in football, it is always a calculated risk, but you keep an eye on what is going on. I knew that Leeds had made a great run from Christmas until the end of the previous season and didn't miss promotion by much. I also knew that Don was doing something because he'd signed Bobby Collins, which I felt was a huge signing. I had a great regard for Bobby as a player, so I thought if Bobby was at the club then there must be something happening. I quickly made up my mind to go.

When I arrived at Leeds United, the players were younger than I expected. I didn't know a great deal about the club, but Gary Sprake, Paul Reaney, Norman Hunter and Billy Bremner was playing. Eddie Gray, Peter Lorimer, Paul Madeley, Terry Cooper, Jimmy Greenhoff and Mick Bates were among young players not yet ready for the first team, but coming on. Then there was Bobby Collins and Jack Charlton, who had experience.

After winning promotion in the 1963/64 season, we went up to the top flight with a reputation of being a hard side and it was justified. In the Second Division, we were a dogged set of lads and did not take any nonsense. A lot of it was exaggerated, but there was some gamesmanship such as holding onto the ball in the corner. It was successful, though it annoyed people. Nowadays you see teams do it all the time, but mud sticks, we got a bad name and it was difficult to shake off.

We surprised people back in the First Division in 1964/65 and maybe ourselves a bit. We ran Manchester United all the way for the title. To get 61 points was normally enough to win the title, but we missed out on goal average. We were a young team, with less ability man for man in relation to United, so to defeat them at Old Trafford in the league and then in the FA Cup semi-finals was a remarkable achievement.

It was clear when I arrived at Leeds United that there was a great team spirit. I'd come from Manchester United who had a lot of star players, but it was not as intimate as it was at Leeds where the players, who had grown up together, genuinely got on. They'd sorted out a number of lads who had not been good for the club. There was a great work ethic and the attention to detail by players, individual coaches Syd Owen and Les Cocker, and manager Don Revie was immense. It was clear that the players wanted to do it.

Over the coming two seasons we made great progress, even if not in terms of honours. We finished runners-up in the league again, reached an FA Cup semi-final, Fairs Cup semi-final and Fairs Cup final. We were maturing, but we played in a certain way, a restricted way. Doing what we did was not a recipe for lasting success, so there had to be a subtle change to be more creative and inventive.

In Europe, we competed with the best. Playing European football, I never thought you needed to adapt that much myself, because wherever you play, you control the ball and pass the ball. When you haven't got it, then you have to get it back. So, whether we played Valencia, Torino or Ferencvaros, it's just a football pitch. Tactics are an overrated thing in football, ultimately, whatever the tactics are, you have to pass the ball, control the ball, score goals and defend your goal. Football is football universally; the Brazilians have a slightly different game, but ultimately it boils down to the same thing.

Missing honours, you have to put down to experience. We were learning all the time and did have misfortune. Against Chelsea in the 1967 FA Cup semi-final, we had a disputed goal disallowed, but we made great progress in Europe. By now Peter Lorimer, Eddie Gray, Paul Madeley and Terry Cooper were in the team. All were younger than the nucleus of the side.

Players need attributes for positions and Don spotted that early on, so the likes of Paul Reaney, Norman Hunter and Terry Cooper all switched positions. All three had qualities to become a professional footballer, then had other qualities to move into positions for the benefit of the team. The further back you are the easier it becomes. Norman and Paul were great defenders anyway, so the switch was relatively easy. With Terry, Don felt he wasn't quite doing it in one position, but felt he could play somewhere else and he did at left-back. Central midfield was my natural position, but I played inside-forward as a kid. At Manchester United, the only place I could get into the team was either midfield or outside-right. Don was honest with me from the start. I told him that I didn't like playing on the wing, but he wanted to have Bobby and Billy in the centre, so I agreed to play on the right.

When Bobby got injured in Turin during a Fairs Cup clash an opportunity to play more centrally arrived and it worked out for me. When I played in the middle at Manchester United, I was 21 and didn't have the experience. At Leeds, I'd had three years playing with Bobby Collins in that position, so by the time I took over I matured enough to handle a very responsible position. At Leeds, I'd pushed in a bit from the right the way we played; I was not isolated on the wing, so was better equipped mentally to do the job. You learn a lot from the likes of Bobby. His will to win was much stronger than most players and he was very positive. Even if we had key players out and things looked dodgy for a game, the thought of not winning never crossed Bobby's mind.

Like Bobby, I had a reputation of being able to look after myself. This dated back to when I was on the end of a nasty challenge at Birmingham City playing for Manchester United. I was out for four months with an ankle injury and realised that relying on the referee for protection would not work. I'd have to get stuck in. It was a different era to the modern game. It was physical and vicious at times, and players like Bobby and me were targets. You either took the stick and risk being put out of a game or responded. I responded.

When I teamed up with Billy, one of us stayed back while the other went forward, but only at the right time. It was a bit like the Lampard and Gerrard conundrum for England these days – except we sorted it out. We had the intelligence to balance up on the football pitch because the ball is in motion all the time. We both scored 115 goals for Leeds. When you look at that statistic, you say, who was the holding player? The holding player was the person at the right time.

Billy was an exceptional player and had the confidence to try things out on the pitch. Most players would not think about it, but Billy had the ability to do it. In our partnership, I was the more boring one in the way I played, but we fed off each other and played little one-twos to get out of tight areas. It happened naturally. You could not practice in training what would happen on the football pitch. It was instant, it was quick and we produced things in difficult situations.

There is a lot of nonsense talked about captaincy. With the players we had, it did not take much captaincy. The main point of a captain is to do it on the pitch. Billy was inspirational because of the things he did on the pitch. Billy was always likely to get a goal. He had a good shot, an instinct for a goal and was a big game player. Billy would not suffer nerves before a match, he would be loud and kidding around while other lads like me would be quiet and more reflective.

During the 1967/68 campaign, we started to turn into a real team. We had a lot of experience, the team was packed with young players coming into their prime, and they had a great attitude. Winning the League Cup was a big thing for us. Originally, the final was two-legged but became more lucrative when it went to Wembley and a place in Europe was at stake. Winning the League Cup proved that we could win. Towards the end of the campaign however, with all the games, we tired and lost out in the FA Cup semi-final for a second successive season and fell away in the league but we did reach the Fairs Cup final, which was delayed to the start of the next season.

During the season, Mick Jones had arrived, really as a replacement for Jimmy Greenhoff, who moved on. Mick was a strong-running player, honest, scored his share of goals and gave us an extra dimension in attack alongside Peter Lorimer who only moved to the right wing when Allan Clarke replaced Mike O'Grady before the 1969/70 season.

In 1968/69 we got off to a flying start, but I picked up an injury in the Fairs Cup final first leg against Ferencvaros, so missed the return in

Budapest. It was a great performance by the lads to come home with the trophy. We now really had a winning mentality and our form carried on despite losing in the league to defending champions Manchester City and Burnley, who had terrific talent.

I regained fitness after a brief spell out, and helped us build an unbeaten run after the 5-1 loss at Burnley. During a superb run, we won 10 out of 11 matches at one stage, including a 6-1 win in the return against Burnley, which was pleasing after the beating we had taken, and a 5-1 triumph at Stoke City. Of more significance though were hard-earned home victories against Newcastle United, Manchester United and Chelsea. In tight games, we had a tremendous never-say-die attitude and it paid dividends repeatedly.

After exiting the FA Cup and Fairs Cup early on for once, we had just one trophy on which to concentrate our efforts. We were determined to succeed. As the season reached the crucial run-in phase just Liverpool, who we defeated earlier in the season at Elland Road, stood in our way of winning a first League championship, the ultimate domestic honour.

Our clash at Liverpool had been postponed until late in the season. Although we were ahead on points, the feeling approaching the run-in, particularly from Liverpool manager Bill Shankly, was that against Manchester City at home and then Arsenal and Everton away, we'd drop points. Liverpool were going well, so this would mean that our clash in the penultimate game of the season at Anfield would be a championship decider.

If you are going to win the league title then you have to deserve to do it. No-one is going to hand it to you on a plate. The tension built as we approached the run-in because games became more and more important. We went into a certain zone, belief is essential. No matter how difficult the match, concentration was at a high level. Despite what Shankly said, we knew that we were capable of winning the matches. I managed to score in wins over Manchester City and Arsenal. We then drew at Everton.

The feeling amongst the lads was that we were nearly there, but there was a lot of tension in our camp. Even Billy, who tended to be the least nervous before games, was keyed up. He found it difficult to sleep and was tenser for this game than the 1965 FA Cup final. We all knew what this match meant.

Before each game in the build up, Don said, if we get anything today lads, we'll win it, but Liverpool kept winning too, so he had to keep saying it. Then we got to the Liverpool game, the real crunch game, and we didn't need telling that if we got anything then we would win it. We had 64 points with two games remaining. It was a huge number, yet we still had not won as Liverpool had 59 points with three games left. It was going right to the end. With Leeds, nothing was easy, but we knew that a point would be enough no matter what Liverpool did in their remaining games. But a point at Anfield was a rare and precious commodity in those days.

The gates were locked long before kick off as 5,000 fans were turned away. The atmosphere was electric and pretty hostile to us. The match was played on a windy night and the pitch was hard and bumpy. We were up to the challenge from kick-off. The conditions suited defences and in the opening minutes, neither team flinched. Early on, the challenges came flying in. Terry Cooper fouled Tommy Smith and Mick Jones was late in a clash with Liverpool keeper Tommy Lawrence. Home fans' anger turned to cheers when Smith gained retribution by body-checking Mick, who needed treatment. The scene was set for a tough battle.

The opening was dour, which was not surprising with so much at stake. We opted to defend and stifle Liverpool. We had a draw mentality going into the game and did not over extend ourselves. It was a question of holding them. Our experience gained in Europe enabled us to get a stranglehold on the match. The tackles were fierce, sometimes ferocious. Anfield was no place for feint hearts.

Ian Callaghan had the first meaningful shot on goal after around 20 minutes, but was well off the mark, then I had a strike at goal, which was parried by Lawrence. Liverpool then wasted a glorious opportunity on the half hour when Bobby Graham broke through, but centre-forward Alun Evans, a £100,000 signing from Wolves, blazed his cross over the bar from six yards.

The frustration from the Kop was noticeable and a good sign for us. Billy almost snatched the lead for us with a deflected shot, but in the main, we were on the defensive as Liverpool probed. We had few anxious moments in the first half, although Paul Madeley had to clear a dangerous attack with Gary out of position close to the break.

In the second half, Evans had two half chances, but was wide again after being set up by Graham and Ian St John. It was tense, but we knew our game plan and so did Liverpool. There was a moment of light relief when the referee, Mr Dimond, stumbled and needed attention from the Liverpool trainer, but the action was soon back on at full tilt.

On the hour, Gary made the save of the match from a rising shot by Callaghan. It would be the closest Liverpool would come to scoring. For a neutral, it was not a classic because there were few chances. But who cares? The result meant everything to us.

With 15 minutes left, you had to do the right things to get the point required. Of course, there is tension, but not in the way that supporters feel it. You can't get too nervous, you have got to be controlled to win. Control the ball, pass the ball, read the game, do the things you have to do. It's no good cracking up, you would not be there in the first place. It's an attitude of mind.

We eventually got a sign from the bench that four minutes remained, then three. Everybody was up tight on the bench, but the game fizzled out. At the final whistle, it was more relief than anything else. After all to win the league it's not the match on the day, but what you have achieved over the season that's won you the trophy. That is why players want to win the Championship rather than the Cup. It's about consistency over a league campaign and we had proved that over 41 matches. Although we had clinched the title at Liverpool, we won it in the other 40 games.

We were all ecstatic. Everyone was jumping around and hugging each other. Before the game Don had said to Billy, "if we win the title tonight take the boys over to the Kop." Billy wasn't too keen, none of us were, but, as we were going back to our dressing room, Don told Billy again to take the lads to the Kop and salute them. Most of the lads were a bit anxious, but Don insisted. As we walked over, the massed fans slowly went quiet. There was an eerie silence and we got more anxious, but then suddenly, someone began to chant 'Champions, Champions, Champions'. Incredibly everyone joined in. We'd won the title at our greatest rivals, but the Liverpool fans were great. They are football people and their reaction showed what good sports there were.

Back in the dressing room, you are caught up in the excitement and the relief of the game, but the feeling dawns that you are Champions. You have done it. Bill Shankly congratulated us and said, "the best team drew." Bill thought right up to the last second that Liverpool would clinch the title, but recognised what it took to win the league.

Don and Bill had great respect for each other, as did the teams. We got stuck into each other playing, but when you speak to the likes of Roger Hunt, Ian St John and Tommy Smith, the respect they have for Leeds is still there.

Back in Leeds, we went to the Queen's Hotel and had a few drinks. We still had to play Nottingham Forest and the record points total was possible, but players don't look at records; that is for when you finish your career. Players want to win trophies. Against Forest, it was a great atmosphere, but a bit of an anti-climax because we were still celebrating. Forest could have scored early on, but we eventually claimed victory when I managed to grab a late goal.

Winning the title, we created numerous club records. Most points (67), most home points (39), most wins (27), most home wins (18), fewest defeats (2), unbeaten at home, 26 goals conceded and only nine of those at home. Thousands turned out to salute us when we paraded the League Championship trophy on an open-top bus through the streets from Elland Road to a civic reception at the town hall the following day. They were unforgettable scenes.

To win the Championship was hard as there was so much competition. It was eight months' hard work in all types of weather. Around eight teams could win it in those days, so it was a big achievement. The satisfaction sank in, but you have to get rid of that because the next season is just around the corner. You are only as good as your last match.

Nothing was too much trouble for Don. His attention to detail, discipline and dedication were his great strengths. Don had a great knowledge of the game. If something happened on a Saturday, however small it may be, he'd put it right on the Monday. You hear a lot about coaching badges, but without knowledge of the game, it means nothing. Where it matters is on the pitch. If we lost a goal on a Saturday, we'd be working on it Monday. Don would say, who should have been here, who was in the wrong position. Don was the only person I came across in football, who did that and without video replays. If you put the little things right, you improve from match to match. If I made a mistake, he made sure I wouldn't do it again.

We did not become a great side until 1968/69 when that championship win confirmed it. Over a decade, no team won more trophies than we did. We've been criticised that we should have won more, which is fair comment in some ways, but unfair in other ways. OK, we lost three out of four FA Cup finals, but it's strange to think that, if we hadn't reached the finals and instead gone out in the third round, we would not have been criticised. It's only because we were knocking on the door to finish runners-up that criticism came our way. It is very difficult for people to appreciate the effort it takes to go with the same attitude after eight years as it was after two or three years. Season after season we were there and knocked on the door. We had our disappointments, but picked ourselves up to start again, then again and again. No other side did it year on year on year. Ultimately we were victims of our own success. We were the first team not to win the league with 61 points in 1964/65 and we lost the title with 64 points to Arsenal in 1970/71. We didn't crack up. Then there was Wolves in 1971/72 when various things happened. Then there was Sunderland in '73 of course. Despite the disappointment, I would not change it. You appreciate the successes when you have comparative failures, there is no doubt about that and all the lads can look back with satisfaction.

What we achieved in 1973/74 does not happen by accident, that is the lads staying together, a will to do it, taking it on the chin, no moaning. When we went onto the pitch, we were capable of beating any team. Whether we did, was another story because we had to play well, but the professionalism of the players and set up was something that I always wanted to be part of as a professional footballer.

EDDIE GRAY
MIDFIELDER 1965–1984

BORN   17th January 1948, Glasgow
SIGNED   January 1965 as apprentice
LEEDS CAREER   579 games, 69 goals
HONOURS   1 Division One Championship, 1 FA Cup, 1 League Cup,
1 Fairs Cup, 12 Scotland caps, 2 Scotland U23 caps
LEFT   Retired May 1984

Eddie was a majestic sight in full flight on the left flank. A prodigious talent
and blessed with sensational skills, Eddie teased, tormented and bamboozled
the best defenders in the country. A member of the Leeds side that won the
League Cup and First Division championship in the late 60s, Eddie reserved
a virtuoso performance for the 1970 FA Cup final and deservedly won the
Man of the Match award. Injuries, though, took a toll forcing him to miss
four European finals and his dozen Scotland caps was scant reward. Eddie
did eventually enjoy an injury-free run in the late '70s and converted to
left-back in 1980.

Leeds United 2 v Burnley 1

Division One
Saturday 4th April 1970

Elland Road
Attendance 24,691

Eddie Gray scores two of the greatest ever goals witnessed at Elland Road

Teams

Don Revie	Managers	Jimmy Adamson
David Harvey	1	Peter Mellor
Terry Yorath	2	John Angus
Paul Peterson	3	Mick Docherty
Paul Madeley	4	Colin Waldron
John Faulkner	5	Martin Dobson
Eddie Gray	6	Sam Todd
Peter Lorimer	7	Frank Casper
Mick Bates	8	Arthur Bellamy
		(Sub. Brian O'Neil)
Albert Johanneson	9	Eric Probert
Chris Galvin	10	David Thomas
Terry Hibbitt	11	Steve Kndon
Gray 10, 71	Scorers	Faulkner (og) 26

Referee: J Taylor

IN 1969/70, I was part of the side that reached the European Cup semi-finals and finished runners-up in the League and FA Cup. Losing to Chelsea in a replay was a heartbreaking end to a season that had promised so much. A week before the final at Wembley, with the title gone, I was one of just three first team regulars that played in an experimental side against Burnley in a league clash. Supporters over 35 years on never tire of reminding me of my goals, the first a 35-yard lob over goalkeeper Peter Mellor and then a solo run through six Burnley players. Supporters say they are among the greatest goals they ever witnessed at Elland Road. Both still give me great satisfaction all these years later and make that match particularly special.

Growing up in Glasgow, football is something that becomes part of you. I used to watch Willie Fernie, Charlie Tully and Bobby Collins play for Celtic with my dad. My favourite player was Willie who played left-wing, but becoming a footballer was not something I thought about too much, although I played for my school team from an early age. People said I was greedy because I liked taking players on and was not put off if I lost the ball. Willie was the same; he'd lose the ball then go on a run past players and score. That is how kids learn. It was the same watching Bobby, the way he swayed his hips to take players out of a game.

I saw Celtic in the 1954, 1955 and 1956 Scottish Cup finals. We beat Aberdeen, then lost to Clyde (my mother was a Clyde supporter, so it didn't go down well) then got beat by Hearts. A year later, I saw Celtic hammer Rangers 7-1 in the Scottish League Cup final. They were fantastic occasions. When Celtic played Rangers, there was always a capacity crowd. The atmosphere when you look back was not nice; it was very hostile, but very exciting. That is how you grew up and it was a religious thing, which wasn't right.

I trained at Celtic Park, but Celtic being Celtic, were very clever. They concentrated on getting Protestant players, as they knew Rangers would not sign a Catholic. They paid little interest in me before it was too late. I could have signed for a number of clubs including Manchester United and Arsenal and I was tempted to join Celtic, who made a big effort once they found out I was set to join Leeds United in 1962, but it was too late. I was not going to change my mind.

I remember watching Manchester United after the Munich air disaster, but I'd actually never heard of Leeds United. Their chief scout in Scotland, John Barr, spotted me and approached my father when I was playing for Glasgow Schoolboys. I met Don Revie, who was a young manager at the time. He was so enthusiastic. I came down to Leeds and fell in love with the place. I came to Leeds United because of Don Revie. His enthusiasm for the football club got to you. Don was a clever man. The year before me, he persuaded Peter Lorimer and Jim McCalliog, who both played for Scottish Schoolboys, to join. You could sense everyone was enjoying it. Unlike the English boys such as Norman Hunter and Paul Reaney, the Scottish boys could not sign as apprentice professionals. We were amateurs, so other clubs could still approach us.

Tommy Docherty took Jim down to Chelsea when he was due to sign professional forms so Don's efforts backfired a bit. There was talk of Celtic coming in for me, but I was happy at Leeds. Becoming a professional footballer was something that happened as I progressed from school to Glasgow Schoolboys to Scottish Schoolboys then Leeds United. Peter and I came down with a lot of publicity. In terms of ability Peter was the main man with Scottish Schoolboys and then I was the next main man.

Leeds United was a great football club to join and there was tremendous banter among the players. At the time, the club had not won anything. They were still in the old Second Division, but there was a belief that Don was building something. Don had a lot of support from club chairman Harry Reynolds to sign up young players. It was something Leeds United had not done before. The club was going places and Harry would be backing Don all the way.

Don was way ahead of his time. People go on about diets today. We used to line up on a morning to drink sherry, eggs and milk, which built us up. He would then give us a steak to take home to our digs. Don also joined in during training sessions. Everything he did was so enthusiastic. If you had a happy football club then you had a fair chance of becoming a successful football club and that is what Leeds United was like in the early '60s.

All these years later when the lads get together at a dinner or function, it's as if I saw them yesterday. It's the same with all the boys. The funny thing about Leeds, and I don't know why it happened, is that many lads who came down from Scotland and didn't make it still settled in Leeds. Don made us all feel at home. Lads went on to play elsewhere, but still came back to live in Leeds. Arthur Graham made his name at Aberdeen, joined Leeds United then went to Manchester United, but now lives in Leeds.

I could have made my first team debut earlier than I did, but I picked up a thigh injury against Sheffield Wednesday Reserves when I was 16. I was playing in the first team within a year, but the injury affected me throughout my career. When I look back, the treatment of injuries was pathetic, but that's progression, I suppose.

One exercise I had involved me kicking a medicine ball in a bath. I had five operations between the ages of 16 and 24 that led to scar tissue and it shortened the muscle, which was my kicking leg. Coming back, if I ran too quick or kicked the ball too hard the muscle went. I learned how to play with it and eventually missed fewer games, but it did hold me back. That's football and its part of the game.

The weekend I made my first team debut, ironically against Wednesday, my younger brother Frank came down to stay with me. I found out the day before the game I'd be playing. I wasn't nervous, I was looking forward to the game. I'd played in big games at different stages of my career, so playing for Leeds United at that particular time was a big game at that age.

As a young player at a club, people think it must be great, but it's not always like that, there are plenty of rivalries. A regular first team player does not want a young upstart coming in to take their place. In my case, Albert Johanneson would not have wanted me to replace him at outside-left. That is why when you go to a football club as a young player, as well as talent, you need a bit of luck along the way and a bit of arrogance about your ability.

Many young boys with potential didn't make it. We were all mates on the ground staff and had a laugh, but when we finished training a few of us kicked the ball around on Fullerton Park, others went down the snooker hall. There is a fine line between making it and not making it. You had to have confidence in your own ability. I believed that I was the best in my position.

Following my debut, I made a handful of appearances before breaking into the side on a regular basis in the 1966/67 season. Don used me in different roles initially. Early on in the season, I scored in a 1-1 draw at Turf Moor playing centre-forward against Burnley. Jim Storrie, Jimmy Greenhoff and Alan Peacock all played the role, but Don was still looking for a long-term solution.

My move to outside-left came about halfway through the 1967/68 campaign. An injury to Bobby Collins in 1965 against Torino saw Johnny

Giles replace him in midfield and partner Billy Bremner. Don obviously looked at the situation with Albert in the side and thought, "Eddie can run." I was quick and could get by people as well as pass a ball from midfield. I think he felt that to take the club forward, we'd be stronger if I could play at outside-left. I'd never played there in my life, but although it was not my natural position, I got a lot of enjoyment playing on the wing.

As a kid, I always tried to take players on. I was also a believer in taking defenders on because once you got past it opened the game up. I could pass and dribble, so if I didn't get past with the ball, I could get past by passing or playing one-twos. Being a midfield player, I got used to being surrounded by people. When your back is to play, you have to be quick to get away from people. I was used to that, so moving positions went smoothly.

Playing out wide, I got plenty of the ball and had one of the best attacking left-backs behind me in Terry Cooper. With Terry getting forward at every opportunity, it took attention off me. Terry moving back from his initial midfield position was great for him because he was coming onto everything and could go beyond me. With me at outside-left and Terry at left-back we had more balance. We weren't the only players to switch position. Paul Reaney and Norman Hunter both converted early on and Paul Madeley would play in every outfield position.

Liverpool was always THE big game. Phil Thompson told me on a radio show that when he first came into the Liverpool side in the early '70s, the players did not even speak about playing Manchester United, the team to beat was Leeds United. That was always the game, Liverpool versus Leeds. There was a rivalry and a friendship between Don Revie and Bill Shankly. To win the championship at Anfield was a wonderful occasion for the football club and players.

The funny thing about football is when people talk about great Leeds players, nobody mentions Mike O'Grady, who played 38 games at outside-right that season. He always reminds me that we were the wingers when we won the league. Mike was a smashing player. Peter played up front with Mick Jones, who joined from Sheffield United in 1967, but missed a number of games. Mike had a great season before injury cost him his place.

When you look back, Peter Lorimer's record was phenomenal because he played the majority of games at outside-right and still finished top scorer by a mile. Peter was a great finisher. The majority were explosive, bang. When he hit a ball you thought, "that's in the back of the net." When he had half a yard, you thought, "there's half a chance here."

The 1969/70 campaign was the start of us being recognised as a great football team. All the lads thought, we are playing some football now. Before, there was a feeling that Leeds was a hard, nasty, over-professional team and even when we won the title, we didn't really get the credit that we deserved. It took until the following season for that to happen. Journalists started saying that we were playing some of the best football the English game had seen. We had power, pace and skill.

Don had strengthened the attack by buying Allan Clarke from Leicester. Don thought, "this is the way I'm going to play." He'd already moved me to outside-left and now moved Peter to outside-right. Allan teamed up with Mick Jones and proved to be a great partnership. Allan had great self-belief and was a great striker. Allan could pass it, control it, was great in the air, quick and had two good feet. Joining Leeds was the making of him as a footballer because everywhere else he was so far ahead. Clarkie was clinical, a Jimmy Greaves-type finisher. When he was one-on-one you thought, "he's going to score." Mick was not as talented as Allan was, but made space for him, took the knocks, never complained and got on with the job.

I can't really recall a game when beforehand I thought we'd get beaten. We were such a formidable outfit. Whatever the weaknesses in our opponents, we had the players to work it out. Don kept juggling the formation, but with respect to anyone else, it revolved around 12 players. Whichever way you looked at it, if I was injured, Don would play three in midfield with Paul Madeley coming in. Paul was always in the team due to injuries or tactics. If everyone had been fit, I'm not sure who would have dropped out, but it never happened.

Winning the league, I think, relaxed Don a bit more. Don had finally done something that he had wanted to achieve. I scored in the Charity Shield curtain raiser when we defeated Manchester City 2-1 and we started the campaign well. By the run-in we were in with a chance of retaining our First Division title and winning the FA Cup and European Cup.

In the FA Cup, we played Manchester United in the semi-finals. It was a huge game and flashed my mind back to 1965 when we defeated them at the same stage. I remember vividly the night of the replay. I was watching it like a schoolboy, thinking, "these Manchester United players are something special," but we won the game. It was unbelievable when Billy scored with a flying back-header. We came through this 1970 semi-final as well after three tough games, with another goal by Billy. We were through to play Chelsea.

Growing up in Scotland, I watched the FA Cup final every year and, at Leeds, I remember watching West Ham defeat Preston North End 3-2 in 1964. The first final I saw live was when Leeds played Liverpool the following year. Seeing everyone walk down Wembley Way was fantastic, then Abide with Me. I'd played in big games, but this was the biggest single game for every footballer.

At Wembley, I remember seeing the pitch beforehand and it looked like a ploughed field. What is remarkable was the standard of play on what was a terrible surface, which had tons of sand poured onto it because of persistent rain and damage caused by the Horse of the Year Show. It was a joke and not like the usual Wembley pitch players looked forward to playing on. That situation would not occur in the modern game.

The biggest single thing I remember about the game was after around five minutes, I thought, "there is no way we cannot win this game." I thought, "it will be a walk in the park," especially after Big Jack scored the first goal. I thought, that's it. Unfortunately we conceded 'that goal' when Gary Sprake let a speculative Houseman shot go under his body, but even then I still thought it was only a matter of time before we scored again. I hit the bar, had another effort brilliantly saved by Peter Bonetti and set up Johnny Giles only for David Webb to clear off the line.

The longer the game went on the more the pitch churned up. The ball had no bounce. All the defenders were troubled when opponents were running at them with the ball. I certainly got more effective as the pitch deteriorated. We took the lead late on through Mick, but instead of killing the game as we would normally do, continued to attack. It had been such an open final, the most attractive for years, but it cost us when Big Jack was penalised for a push on Osgood and from the free-kick, Hutchinson headed home. Neither side could force a winner in extra-time.

Much has been written about my performance and the problems I caused right-back David Webb. He was better suited to a central defensive role and was not helped by Tommy Baldwin, who came in for the injured Alan Hudson. Webb switched positions with Ron Harris for the replay at Old Trafford and, as he has stated over the years, was determined to stop me playing. Although I was not as dangerous as at Wembley we should have won after Mick gave us the lead. Osgood's equaliser and Webb's extra-time winner was devastating.

In the European Cup, we reached the semi-finals where we faced Celtic, but overall they were the better team. At Elland Road, it could have gone either way, but we did not play as well as we were capable of and lost 1-0.

At Hampden Park, we played quite well. Billy scored a great goal, but Celtic played better. They were not a better team than we were but overall deserved to win.

We would ultimately miss out in all three major competitions yet the team received praise for our 'glorious failure', but we all found it hard at the time to savour the praise. This is why I did not get much satisfaction from being voted Man of the Match in the FA Cup final.

The 1969/70 league campaign had begun well and once again, we were among the contenders. The season was concertinaed due to the World Cup finals in Mexico and with us being involved in all the competitions, fixture congestion was inevitable. I missed a couple of months after New Year, but by my return in a 5-1 win over West Brom we were in shake up for the treble. We did remarkably well to keep going, but something had to give. It proved firstly to be the league.

Four days after defeating Manchester United in the FA Cup semi-finals, Don sent out a 'shadow' team to face Derby County, which signalled the end of our league ambitions for a season and it stayed that way for the final four fixtures. When we ran out to play Burnley in our penultimate home game, it was our fifth game in 10 days. It was also our third match in four days, which included the European Cup semi-final first leg defeat. And they complain about having too much football today!

Our 2-1 victory over Burnley in the league gave me much more satisfaction than my performance against Chelsea a week later, even though it had no bearing on honours. We played a 'shadow' side with the FA Cup final coming up. Apart from me, only Peter Lorimer and Paul Madeley were first team regulars. Many reserves got a taste of first team action. It would prove to be a game that I will never forget because of two goals I scored.

With so many first teamers rested, it was an opportunity for the reserves to make a mark and for John Faulkner it was a special day as he made his first team debut. John had impressed for Sutton United when they faced Leeds in an FA Cup tie during the season. We won 6-0, but John shone sufficiently for Don to sign him as a possible long-term replacement for Big Jack. I played in central midfield. The crowd was poor [under 25,000 as opposed to the 45,000 who had attended the previous home game], but with the Cup final coming up it was understandable and many probably stayed at home to watch the Grand National.

With all the changes, it took us time to settle and Burnley had the opening chances, Steve Kindon and Frank Casper going close.

Opportunities came for both sides; John almost got a debut goal with a volley from a Terry Hibbitt centre before a shot by Albert Johanneson just missed the target. Arthur Bellamy went close for Burnley before I opened the scoring.

Most supporters think the second goal was the best, but I prefer the first one, which came when the ball broke to me from a headed clearance by a Burnley defender following a left-wing cross from Chris Galvin. I noticed Mellor off his line, but was not sure if I could set myself up to exploit it. The key was my first touch; there was no margin for error. Two Burnley defenders were closing in, so it had to be perfect or the chance would have gone. It gave me the most pleasure of all the goals I scored for Leeds.

The goal was something I had to think about quickly. If you look at it on video, Mellor is not very far off his line, so as the ball came to me, I had to control it quickly. When I controlled it and looked up, I thought, "there's a chance here." The execution of it was spot on for what I wanted to achieve.

Burnley attempted to hit back and after keeping us under pressure without having any clear openings, John marked his debut in the worst way by scoring an own goal when he turned in a dangerous cross from Eric Probert. The remainder of the half brought no more goals.

On the resumption, Kindon and Albert [Johanneson] both went close to scoring before David Harvey in our goal was forced into two expellant saves to deny Kindon again and Martin Dobson. Terry Hibbitt was causing Burnley a lot of problems from the left wing, but we could not find the finishing touch. With around 20 minutes to go, I scored our second goal. I'd scored a similar one against Derby County in a League Cup semi-final when I beat four or five players before toe-poking it in. Close control was something that came naturally to me.

My dribble started almost on Burnley's own goal line, just outside the 18-yard box and initially took me away from goal with Albert on the ground. Most dribbles start near the half way line, but this one started much closer to the opponents' goal. You don't go running towards the corner flag thinking, "I'm going to score here." It was something that just happened. When I picked up the ball, trying to score was the furthest thing from my mind. All I was trying to do was control the ball, make an opening to create something and then let it develop from there. As I made my way inside the box, things started to open up. As I got into position, I thought, "if I can manoeuvre this, I could knock it in." It just happened.

Burnley put us under a lot of pressure in the closing stages and were unfortunate not to equalise as David [Harvey] saved point black from

O'Neil before Dobson and Casper both struck the woodwork. It was a close run thing in the end, but we held out for a satisfying win. It was not one for the record books and did not win any trophies, but is remembered all these years on by many fans present that day.

A week later, I played in my first FA Cup final. You have to give Chelsea credit for the way they battled away, but all I could think of was that we should have won the Cup. It was so disappointing. To come so close was heartbreaking. Europe was great, but as a player, you wanted to win a League Championship and FA Cup winners medal. I had one but not the other at that stage, although we did rectify that a couple of years later.

To be part of a football club that was at the top, playing with great players and knowing at times that we were playing some of the greatest football was for me what it was all about. People talk about the Southampton game in 1972, but a few weeks before we thrashed Manchester United with Charlton, Best and co. The win over United was the best team performance I recall. Nobody could remember when they had been defeated as comprehensively as we beat them. Our games were always tight, but no team could have lived with us that day. One enduring image I recall is a photograph of Peter and me by a corner flag during a break for an injury. We look so relaxed. Bobby Charlton's face at the end told its own story. Don told Mick Bates in the dug out, "This is as good as it gets". Don was right. That game may have been our best performance, but my goals against Burnley have also stood the test of time, which is immensely satisfying.

It seems such a long time ago that I first came down to Elland Road and the car park was black ash. When I look at the development of the football club, you are glad to be part of it, whether good or bad. It was a great experience and I enjoyed every minute of it. I've read the history of the club and Leeds United has always experienced difficult times, even going back to the time when the club had to reform when Leeds City was thrown out of the Football League in 1919. In Big John Charles's era, there was little success, then Don Revie arrived and the traditions started.

I was fortunate to join in 1962, when the real tradition of the football club was born. People all over the world soon discovered Leeds United. We didn't win as many trophies as we should have done, but between 1968 and 1974 we won six, which was more than any other club during that time and there were some great teams around like United, Man City, Liverpool, Chelsea and Arsenal. We showed tremendous character to bounce back from disappointments over a long period. To be a part of that was fantastic.

ALLAN CLARKE
FORWARD 1969–1978

BORN   31st July 1946, Short Heath, Nr Willienhall
SIGNED   June 1969 from Leicester City; £165,000
LEEDS CAREER   366 games, 151 goals
HONOURS   1 Division One Championship, 1 FA Cup, 1 Fairs Cup,
18 England caps, 6 England U23 caps
LEFT   Transferred to Barnsley, June 1978

Allan was one of the most feared strikers of his generation. An assassin, 'Sniffer' Clarke could waltz around a goalkeeper with nonchalant ease, catch a defender for pace, or place a shot or header into the net with deadly accuracy. A £165,000 British record transfer fee brought him to Leeds United where he proved to be the final piece of Don Revie's great side. Allan enjoyed his finest years at Elland Road, scoring crucial goals to help Leeds win the Fairs Cup and First Division championship, but his flying header against Arsenal in the 1972 FA Cup final, when he won the Man of the Match award, is the most cherished by Leeds supporters. Player of the Year in 1972/73 and top-scorer on four occasions, Allan is United's third highest ever goal scorer.

Arsenal 0 v Leeds United 1

FA Cup final
Saturday 6th May 1972

Wembley Stadium
Attendance 100,000

Leeds United finally triumph in the FA Cup

Teams

Bertie Mee	Managers	Don Revie
Geoff Barnett	1	David Harvey
Pat Rice	2	Paul Reaney
Bob McNab	3	Paul Madeley
Peter Storey	4	Billy Bremner
Frank McLintock	5	Jack Charlton
Peter Simpson	6	Norman Hunter
George Armstrong	7	Peter Lorimer
Alan Ball	8	Allan Clarke
John Radford	9	Mick Jones
(Sub. Ray Kennedy)		
George Graham	10	Johnny Giles
Charlie George	11	Eddie Gray
	Scorers	Clarke 53

Referee: D Smith

DURING MY NINE YEARS at Leeds United, there were so many highs. It was such a pleasure, because there was so much ability in the side. But selecting just one game from the many glorious memories for me is easy. Although I was part of teams that won the First Division title and Fairs Cup, our FA Cup final win at Wembley in 1972 will always stand out. I'd experienced the heartbreak of losing in 1970 with Leeds, this time would be different. Scoring the winning goal would also make it extra special.

I enjoyed every minute of my childhood. Christmas was always special, because I'd get a new football strip. I was always out kicking a ball in the back yard, on a local football field or at school. If there was no football, we'd roll up a newspaper or use a tennis ball. School reports always said the same. "If Allan showed as much interest in work as football, he would be top of the class."

I was the third eldest of seven children. When it came to the boys, mum and dad accepted that football dominated our lives. Incredibly, Frank, Derek, Kelvin, Wayne and myself all played the game professionally. The Clarke brothers made their mark.

West Brom was our team. My hero was centre-forward Ronnie Allen. The FA Cup final was the highlight each season. The first one I watched was in 1954 when dad bought our first television. I remember Ronnie scoring twice as West Brom beat Preston 3-2. Like all football-mad kids, I dreamt of scoring the winning cup final goal at Wembley one day.

My football journey started at New Invention Infant Junior School and Short Heath Secondary Modern School before I represented South East Staffordshire District and Birmingham County Boys. In 1962, I joined Walsall as an apprentice, in preference to Aston Villa, as I felt I'd get a break in the first team there quicker. During the 1962/63 campaign, Walsall suffered relegation to the Third Division, but I made my first team debut at 17 against Reading.

In 1964/65, I top scored with 23 goals and was voted Player of the Year. It was a tremendous honour. Scoring goals was something that came naturally. Most were the result of instinctive reactions. I trained myself to be alert around the box. Sometimes you run away from a defender to gain that vital split second; you may get the ball in an open space, you may not, but you've got to be alert in case a chance comes.

At the start of the new campaign, I signed my first professional contract and hit the headlines when I scored a last minute penalty to win a League Cup clash against QPR. Supporters carried me shoulder high off the pitch. I scored another penalty when we caused an FA Cup shock to knock out First Division Stoke City. Both were memorable occasions so early in my career.

In March 1966, I joined First Division Fulham for a club record fee of £37,500. Household names at Fulham included Johnny Haynes, George Cohen and Bobby Robson. I was delighted because Fulham was a friendly club. The chairman was comedian Tommy Trinder. I was in awe the first time I met Tommy because I'd only seen him on the Sunday Night at the London Palladium television show. Tommy was terrific and always mocked my Black Country accent.

I made my debut as a substitute, ironically against Leeds. Fulham lost 3-1. Then I made my first full appearance in a rearranged game at Elland Road. We were delighted to win with a 'Pancho' Pearson goal. There was a step-up in ability playing against the likes of Bremner, Charlton, Hunter and Giles; they were class. Don Revie told me when I joined Leeds he had made a mental note that I wasn't afraid to mix-it. He must have seen it fom those games against his side.

Life was hectic because apart from moving to London, I married my fiancée Margaret after returning early from Fulham's post-season Far East tour. Fulham made a poor start in 1966/67, but we did get a 2-2 draw at defending champions Liverpool and I got both goals. Scoring is always special, but getting two at Anfield was amazing. One in particular was memorable because I went on a mazy run from inside Liverpool's half before slipping it past Tommy Lawrence. Bill Shankly said it was one of the best goals he'd seen at Anfield, which was a great compliment.

We avoided relegation. I bagged 29 goals, including a hat-trick against Newcastle United. I also scored four goals on my England U23 debut when we crushed Wales U23 8-0. Following another terrible start in 1967/68, Bobby Robson succeeded Vic Buckingham as manager, but relegation was inevitable. Manchester United bid a British record of £150,000 for me. Bobby said he would not stand in my way. I met Matt Busby and agreed to join during the close season.

I thought that was that.

I finished as Fulham's top-scorer again and on FA Cup final eve lined up for England v Young England. Before the game, Bobby informed me

Leicester City had matched Manchester United's bid and their Club officials were at the game. Out of courtesy, I met Leicester manager Matt Gillies and realised that I wanted to play for him. I signed a three-year contract.

I rang Matt Busby, who was disappointed, but wished me well. Supporters are still amazed I turned Manchester United down, especially as they were about to win the European Cup. But I thought they had peaked and in fact they won nothing for a decade, while I had the most successful period of my career. The fee didn't bother me, but it put me in the spotlight. I was the most expensive British footballer ever, which made me a marked man, but I was ready for the challenge.

At Leicester, I scored on my debut at QPR, but following a 7-1 defeat at Everton, the board sacked Matt Gillies' assistant Bert Johnson. Matt resigned in protest. I was stunned and went round to Matt's house with Willie Bell to persuade him to change his mind, but he stuck to his principles. Frank O'Farrell was appointed manager, but we did not get on from the start. Leicester struggled in the league, but reached the FA Cup final when I volleyed a winner against West Brom in the semi-final.

Reaching Wembley was a fantastic achievement and a major ambition of mine. We faced Manchester City, but for some reason Frank picked me to play in midfield after I'd played as a striker all season. We played well and I picked up the Man of the Match award, but lost 1-0 to a Neil Young goal. After the defeat, we played our final league games, but failed to avoid the drop. So I'd been relegated twice in successive seasons!

There was a lot of speculation about clubs coming in for me, but first I joined England's South America tour to prepare for the 1970 World Cup. On my return, Leicester informed me they had accepted a British record bid of £165,000 from League title winners Leeds United. I believed in my own ability, was single-minded, wanted to be the best and challenge for trophies. I now had a chance.

Over the seasons, I'd discovered that beating Leeds was some achievement. Before a match, the manager of whichever club I played for would say, if you try playing their type of football, they'll murder you, so rough them up a bit. However, whether you played them at football or tried to rough them up, they normally stuffed you. It was great to be playing for them instead of facing them.

I made my Leeds debut against Manchester City in the Charity Shield. We won 2-1. Supporters gave me a tremendous welcome. We had a great rapport and it has never changed. As for my league debut against Tottenham Hotspur, I was determined to make the most of my opportunity. We won 3-1 and I scored a goal, just beating Pat Jennings to a through ball before nodding it over him. I remember the headlines: THE £165,000 GOAL. I'd arrived.

My first season was so different to anything I'd experienced before because we went for the treble. In the league, Everton were the main challengers for the title. In the FA Cup, it took three tough games to get past Manchester United in the semi-finals before Billy Bremner came up trumps. In the European Cup, we faced Celtic in the semi-finals, but had serious fixture congestion.

First, our league hopes disappeared, then we should have buried Chelsea at Wembley, but drew 2-2. Celtic edged our European Cup tie, but I'd have loved to play them a couple of years later when we hit our peak. In the FA Cup final replay, Chelsea proved resilient and won in extra time. During the run-in tiredness crept in, but you put it to the back of your mind. At the time, we simply took each match as it came. It's an old cliché, but that's all you could do. Some people said we'd had a bad season. The majority of players would go though an entire career without coming close to what we achieved; and that was my first season. I loved it.

I'd scored 26 goals in all competitions to finish joint top scorer with Mick Jones. I was delighted. I had also acquired a nickname. Before a game, as usual we watched Football Focus on Grandstand when presenter Sam Leach featured me. He said, now watch how Allan Clarke sniffs out goals. The lads gave me some stick. I was forever more known as 'Sniffer'.

There is pressure on goalscorers, but it never affected me. The bigger the stage the more I loved it. If I missed, I thought, "I'll tuck away the next one." As a striker, you have to be confident in your ability to score. At Leeds, I developed as an all-round striker and like all the lads was able to look after myself. Facing the likes of Chopper Harris, Nobby Stiles and Tommy Smith was always a battle, but my attitude was I'll give as good as I get. My opposite number may kick me, but they had better watch out if they came back again for another go. I found that if I gave the centre-half some stick, they backed off, which gave me room to play.

Back home after the World Cup finals in Mexico, where I scored on my full England debut against Czechoslovakia to win the game 1-0, Leeds prepared for the new campaign. Pre-season training was always tough, but I found it easier than most because I put so little weight on. When we started the cross-country run, I'd be motoring while some of the others that had indulged over the summer struggled big time.

Nothing was routine at Leeds; everything had a purpose. In training, our five-a-side and eight-a-side games were particularly competitive. We'd practice situations from throw-ins, wall passing, all sorts. Then we'd switch to shooting; and that meant everyone. I also practiced one-on-one's, which was a big part of my game.

The night before a match, we played carpet bowls or bingo. Pundits laughed, but it helped us relax. At our team talk, the gaffer went through dossiers on our opponents. Then, before a match, we all had our particular superstitions. I always put my shirt on first, then, slips, shorts, socks and boots. Finally I'd get any plasters and tie-ups I needed. I liked going out of the dressing room last, but at Leeds; Big Jack ran out last, so I was second last until he retired.

I was delighted to be at Elland Road. The players were so ambitious it was frightening. You could sense nothing came before the team and no player was the star. I loved the team spirit in the dressing room and could not believe how fit I became. The players had a different mentality to previous team-mates. They didn't know the meaning of the word 'defeat'.

At previous clubs, I was a winner, but some players would be laughing in the bath after a defeat. I could not accept that. I liked a laugh and a joke, but I took my football seriously. Leeds lost less than other clubs did, but after a defeat, the dressing room would be like a morgue. The players had a winning mentality.

During the 1970/71 campaign, we led the league all season until we entertained West Brom. We lost 2-1, but West Brom's second goal, which looked offside, saw fans invade the pitch. Referee Ray Tinkler required a police escort. It was the worst refereeing decision of my career. We won our remaining games, but Arsenal won the title in the last match enabling them to clinch a famous double that should never have been possible.

Our FA Cup campaign ended when Colchester caused a major FA Cup shock by knocking us out 3-2 at Layer Road. We now had only the Fairs Cup to aim for and played Juventus in the final. The first leg in Italy was abandoned because of torrential rain and in the replayed game; we played brilliantly to draw 2-2. In the return, I opened the scoring before Pietro Anastasi equalised. There were chances at both ends, but we won the trophy on the new away goals rule. I was delighted for the lads. This triumph was extra-special for me because it was my first major honour.

In 1971/72, we played some of the best football ever witnessed at Elland Road. It became a fortress. We watched opponents pass our dressing room door looking beaten before they went onto the pitch. Mike Summerbee once told me they'd just thumped Tottenham. Players were chatting in a suitably upbeat mood in the dressing room, when someone asked whom they had next week, Leeds was the answer; deathly silence engulfed the room.

During a purple patch, we roasted Manchester United 5-1 and then thrashed Southampton 7-0. Every boy starting out in football should watch a video of that Southampton match. I believe our performance was as near perfection from 11 players that you could get. There were great goals, tremendous saves, wonderful pieces of individual skill; you name it, it was in that 90 minutes of football. Our sixth goal summed up our display. Norman Hunter , yes central defender Norman Hunter, made it with brilliant left wing play before crossing for Big Jack to head home. Our two central defenders combining to score illustrated just how much we were on top. When we kept possession late on at 7-0, commentators said we were taking the Mickey. We weren't. Our instructions were to keep out of trouble and avoid injury. We played superbly.

In the FA Cup, losing to Colchester the previous season made us more determined to progress. I missed a third round win against Bristol Rovers, but like all the lads looked forward to the fourth round draw, which took place on a Monday lunchtime. After training, we crammed around a radio. My feeling was firstly disappointment. There was no tougher clash than Liverpool at Anfield, but it didn't take long to relish the challenge. It was the tie of the round.

In front of a packed house, we defended well to earn a replay, which, due to an industrial dispute, kicked-off in the afternoon. There was an electric atmosphere inside Elland Road. Fans scaled the Scratching Shed, others perched on top of the Old Peacock Pub. No-one wanted to miss this match. I had been getting stick from the press about my overall game, so was delighted to grab both goals in a 2-0 win.

For my first goal, Billy played a great ball in. I reacted quickest to put the ball past the boy Clemence. For my second, I picked the ball up just inside Liverpool's half and left Tommy Smith on his backside. The next player was Larry Lloyd. I dropped a shoulder and went past him. Approaching the penalty area, I beat Chris Lawler and faced Clemence, who tried to narrow the angle. Realising that he would expect me to curl it in at the far post I went for the near post. Clemence gave me no more than a yard, but I hit the ball sweetly and squeezed it past him. As an individual goal it was one of the best I scored.

Two Johnny Giles strikes were enough to see off Cardiff City in round five. We wore stocking tags for a quarter-final clash against Tottenham and went through a planned training routine before kick-off. It was a bit of razzamatazz. We got criticism from sections of the media, but supporters loved getting the tags at the end of a game and today it is normal to warm up as a team. After going a goal down to Tottenham when Gary Sprake made a dreadful error, I scrambled an equaliser before Big Jack scored the winner with a trademark header.

The week before our semi-final clash with Birmingham City, Terry Cooper broke a leg at Stoke City, which was devastating, but Paul Reaney slotted in at right-back while Paul Madeley switched to left back. One other change saw the gaffer give David Harvey his big first team opportunity. At times, I think, Don was too loyal, but that was his style. He knew his best team and wanted to stick to it, but finally he lost patience with Gary.

Birmingham were in the Second Division and tried to psyche us out by copying our pre-match routine, but it backfired. It was a shambles. Midway through the first half Peter pinged over a long ball, I nodded it across and Jonah [Mick Jones] popped it in. Peter then added a second. It was over by half time. Jonah scored a third. The result was never in doubt.

Reaching Wembley is so important to a footballer because everyone wants to play at the Twin Towers. I experienced winning and losing semi-final dressing rooms and the difference is immense. When the referee blows the whistle at the end of a semi-final and you know you're at Wembley, the feeling is fantastic.

As Cup final preparations began, we were still involved in the title shake-up alongside Derby County, Manchester City and Liverpool. With Derby a point clear, the FA ruled our final match at Wolves should take place 48 hours after the Cup final against Arsenal.

The build up to Wembley was frantic. Apart from organising tickets, we recorded a Cup final song and got our match-day suits. I'm still not sure which was more embarrassing. Our record 'Leeds, Leeds, Leeds' is now known as 'Marching on Together' and has effectively become the club song. We travelled to London on the Thursday and trained at a local park. I was doubtful along with Eddie Gray and Johnny Giles, but we all passed fitness tests. The night before the game, we played the usual bingo and carpet bowls before watching a video of our 7-0 win over Southampton. The gaffer's friend Herbert Warner was cracking jokes. Herbert was great for morale. We were relaxed and ready.

Arsenal had won the double a year before and like us had a team full of household names. The only possible chink was goalkeeper Geoff Barnett, who was in for regular keeper Bob Wilson, who'd injured himself in their victory over Stoke in the semi-final. I felt we had the edge, though, and believed that finally this would be our year. I wasn't too worried about our 'second string' goalkeeper being between our posts as he was there on merit having been chosen by the manager, rather than as a result of an injury. In fact, David Harvey was a brave goalkeeper, agile, a terrific shot-stopper, handled the ball well, kept good angles and commanded his penalty box.

My partners in crime up front were simply the best around. Eddie Gray is the most naturally gifted footballer I played with. Eddie could do anything with a football, his dribbling skills were unbelievable and he could unlock any defence. People talk about George Best, Eddie had as much ability.

Peter Lorimer had awesome shooting power. He could really leather a ball but was also quick, strong, had great balance and produced pinpoint crosses. Peter was a winger, not a central striker; the number of goals he scored was amazing. Mick Jones was the best striking-partner I played with for club or country. We developed a telepathic understanding. Pundits compared us to the likes of Toshack and Keegan (Liverpool), Radford and Kennedy (Arsenal), Chivers and Gilzean (Tottenham) and Osgood and Baldwin (Chelsea). None touched us.

Jonah was the target man and chased any lost cause. His strength and stamina amazed me. He had terrific close control and held the ball up, while I looked for space to support him. If I was being man-marked, I'd go deep to pick balls up. Any crosses coming into the box, one of us would attack the near post; the other would peel off to the back-stick. Jonah was a brilliant header of the ball and scored his share of goals. Most times I scored Mick played a part.

On Cup final morning, the gaffer kept our routine the same. After the main team talk and pre-match meal, we watched part of Cup Final Grandstand, then set off for Wembley. When the coach turned into Wembley Way, it was a fantastic sight. Supporters were everywhere. Once at the stadium I felt at home. I loved playing at Wembley. We had a walk on the pitch; I checked both penalty areas for divots before television reporters interviewed us.

Back in the dressing room, the gaffer gave his final instructions then had a quick word with each of us. As always, he said to me, "Allan, if you're left one-on-one with the goalkeeper just shake your body, go past him and put it in the net." The gaffer always had confidence in me.

Waiting in the tunnel, I just wanted to get going. Peter Simpson tried to psyche me out. I remember thinking, "this is it." The gaffer led us out into the wall of sound that greets you. We passed a parade to commemorate the Centenary Final on our stroll to the half-way line. It was fantastic. After the presentations, when we ran to our supporters, the tension drained away.

In an explosive opening, I was penalised for fouling Alan Ball and Bob McNab was booked for a late tackle on Peter Lorimer. The weather was red-hot and, although I was fit, after five or ten minutes I was thinking, "Christ, I need another lung here," but then I got my second wind and was fine. Arsenal had early chances. David Harvey made a good save from Frank McLintock, while Paul Reaney cleared a Ball volley off the line.

We also created opportunities. Jonah had an effort scrape a post whilst Peter had an instinctive 20-yard strike fumbled around the post by Geoff Barnett. Our last chance of the opening period came just before half-time when I deflected Peter's cross-cum-shot onto the bar. I'm amazed it didn't knock my head off, but it was close.

Although no goals had been scored, we had edged the half. Billy and Johnny were dictating play in midfield over Ball and George Graham, while Big Jack and Norman had John Radford and Charlie George well shackled. Jonah and I had also caused problems. In the dressing room, the gaffer told us to carry on as we were. We had been the better side and he felt the goal would come.

He was right. Eight minutes into the second half, we scored and it's a moment I'll never forget. A ball was played towards me near the half-way line. McLintock was marking me. As I attempted to get away, Frank pushed me. I tried to stay on my feet, but fell over. Frank trod on my fingers, it didn't half hurt. Ball got the ball and played it forward, Big Jack intercepted it. We were now on the attack.

Jack gave the ball to Paul Madeley, who played a simple pass forward to Peter. I then remember Billy passing me to join the attack. Peter played it to Jonah down the right flank, and I thought, I've got to get into the box here. As Jonah took on Bob McNab, I was on the edge of the box. Mick worked marvels and crossed the ball. As it was coming towards me, I thought, "volley, right foot volley," and I fancied it. Then all of a sudden as the ball's coming across it started to dip and I realised it wasn't going to reach me, so I thought, "dive." You only have a second to make your mind up, so I just took off and headed it. I knew it was going in, and obviously, it fitted in the corner just nicely.

Over the years, I've lost count how many people have asked me about the goal and introduced me to their children who weren't even born in 1972. It means so much to Leeds United supporters. It's a very special memory in my footballing career. Ever since, whenever we play Arsenal at Elland Road, supporters sing 'Who put the ball in the Arsenal net? Allan, Allan. Who put the ball in the Arsenal net? Allan Allan Clarke'. That's a wonderful feeling.

Arsenal weren't finished yet and came forward with Charlie George hitting the bar, but we were in control. Big Jack, Peter, Jonah and Eddie all went close. We should have won more comprehensively.

At the final whistle, it was an incredible feeling. We hugged one another and then all of a sudden, I noticed Jonah lying in Arsenal's penalty area. Les Cocker and Doc Adams were attending to him. I remember Jonah going down, but it proved to be the last action of the match. I didn't realise he was still down. I went over. It was obviously a bad injury, but I was told to join the lads who were lining up to get our medals.

Walking up to get my medal was marvellous. Seeing Billy receive the FA Cup from the Queen and show it to our fans is something I'll never forget. It was great to be voted Man of the Match and I was presented with the trophy when I walked down the steps. Then Jonah went up for his medal holding his arm limply by his side, in obvious pain. I was going to take him, but Norman jumped in ahead of me. The lap of honour was fantastic. It was one of those days when you didn't want to leave the field.

Back in the dressing room, the FA Cup was filled with champagne and we all had a drink. There was relief and joy mixed together. The only sad sight was Jonah, who was resting on a bench in the corner before going to hospital. I sat with him for a while.

Within an hour of the final whistle, the gaffer said, "right lads, let's get moving, we're going to the hotel because we have a big match on Monday." We drove to the Mount Hotel near Wolverhampton and had dinner. Derek Dougan presented me with the Golden Boot for scoring the winning goal. We then watched Match of the Day.

On the Monday, we lost 2-1 to Wolves and with it went our dreams of the double. The FA's insistence that the game take place so close to the Cup final cost us. There was simply no time to recover. In the dressing room, we were inconsolable. Looking back, though, no-one can take away the feelings we had after winning the FA Cup.

My final years at Leeds brought more highs and lows. We reached the FA Cup final again in 1973, but it wasn't to be as Sunderland caused a major upset. A few days later, I missed our European Cup Winners' Cup final defeat by AC Milan when the referee was suspended over bribery allegations.

His display was diabolical. It was a double blow, but as usual, we dusted ourselves down and bounced back.

Winning a First Division title was still a burning ambition for me. I'd by now finished a runner-up three times and before 1973/74, pundits wrote off our chances. The gaffer said, "let's see if can we go through a whole season unbeaten." It was certainly a different pre-season pep talk. Following a record-equalling 29-match unbeaten run, we stuttered after losing an really unbelievable match at Stoke 3-2, but eventually clinched the title. Claiming a championship medal was fantastic. We'd proved we were the best over a season. That is the ultimate accolade for any professional footballer.

That campaign proved to be the gaffer's last at Leeds as he took up the FA's offer to become England manager. Brian Clough took over at Elland Road, but lasted 44 days. Jimmy Armfield arrived as our attention turned to the European Cup. This was our last crack at the biggest prize in Europe. We played well in early rounds and overcame mighty Barcelona in the semi-final. But in the final against Bayern Munich, some questionable refereeing andtwo breakaway goals denied us victory. It was heartbreaking.

At Leeds, we did not win as much silverware as we might have done. To win a Cup final, the best team doesn't always win. You need a bit of luck and we did not always get that. Winning honours was everything to players of my era. We wanted to play football and got paid for doing it. Now it seems players firstly play for the money, then football, which is sad. I was fortunate to play for one of the greatest club teams this country has seen or is likely to see. As a one-off occasion, the FA Cup victory over Arsenal was the most memorable triumph. Supporters still ask me what it was like to win the FA Cup. I tell them it was great. We may have only won it just the once, but we won the big one, the Centenary final.

PETER LORIMER
RIGHT-WING 1962–1979/1983-1985

BORN   14th December 1946, Dundee
SIGNED   March 1962 as apprentice/from Vancouver Whitecaps December 1983
LEEDS CAREER (two spells) 705 games, 238 goals
HONOURS   2 Division One Championships, 1 FA Cup, 1 League Cup,
2 Fairs Cups, 21 Scotland caps, 2 Scotland U23 caps
LEFT   Transferred to Toronto Blizzard, March 1979/Free transfer to
Whitby Town, December 1985

Peter is the most prolific goalscorer in Leeds United's history. He was a
prodigious schoolboy talent and became the clubs youngest debutant. Peter
was dangerous from anywhere in an opponents half and once scored from the
half-way line. His power made him a natural penalty expert and he scored 32
spot-kicks, second only to Johnny Giles. Not only a goal scorer, Peter spread
play with superb accuracy, creating many goals for colleagues with pinpoint
crosses from the right flank. One of only five players to make over 700 appearances for Leeds, but for a spell away in Canada, 'Hotshot' Lorimer would
have claimed this record, on top of his record goal scoring achievements.

Barcelona 1 v Leeds United 1   (Leeds win 3-2 on aggregate)

European Cup Semi-final second leg
Wednesday 23rd April 1975

Camp Nou, Barcelona
Attendance 110,000

Leeds United claim a momentous draw to reach the European Cup final.

Teams

Rinus Michels	Managers	Jimmy Armfield
Salvador Sadurni	1	David Stewart
Mario Marinho	2	Trevor Cherry
Francisco Gallego	3	Frank Gray
Miquel Bianqueti	4	Billy Bremner
Jesus Antonio De La Cruz	5	Gordon McQueen
Johann Neeskens	6	Norman Hunter
Carlos Rexach	7	Paul Madeley
Juan Carlos Heredia	8	Allan Clarke
Johan Cruyff	9	Joe Jordan
Jan Miguel Asensi	10	Terry Yorath
(Sub. Joaquim Rife)		
Manuel Clares	11	Peter Lorimer
Clares 69	Scorers	Lorimer 8
	Sent Off	McQueen 71

Referee: E Linemayer

THE EUROPEAN CUP was the trophy Don Revie always wanted to win and we came close in 1970 when Celtic defeated us in the semi-final. When Don left in 1974, the players remaining from the Celtic clash had one last shot and much of our motivation in 1974/75 was down to that. We wanted to win it for the gaffer and ourselves. European football suited our style of play and we easily made the semi-finals, where we faced Barcelona. We travelled to the Nou Camp with a goal advantage, but Barcelona had an away goal. It was massive challenge and they were favourites with most pundits, but I was confident we could get a result. Our 1-1 draw for me was the highlight of our European clashes over a decade.

Football was always something that came easy to me, which was why from day one I thought I had a chance of making it as a pro. You must have self-belief to succeed. My love of the game probably came from my Uncle Paddy, who lived in Fife and supported Hibernian, so I saw them play quite a lot. Uncle Paddy was a reasonable footballer and used to take me out onto a field at the back of our house and we'd kick the ball about.

My parents, especially my mum, as my dad worked away a lot, encouraged me. She liked her football then and still does. Mum is in her late 80s, but still watches every match that she can on television. Whenever we speak, she always talks about the latest games.

In my hometown, there was Dundee and Dundee United. I watched both play, but not that much because most Saturdays were spent playing football in the morning for my school and in the afternoon for the local boy's club. Every spare minute I had during the winter was spent playing football, and, living by the seaside in the summertime, we were either swimming or fishing.

One season I scored 176 goals for Stobswell School and developed a reputation for my shooting. The power I generated was natural. I never worked on it. Timing, rhythm and technique were important, but it was something I could just do. I represented Dundee Schools and Scotland Schoolboys. Around 40 clubs were after me. The row of cars outside my parent's house was amazing. All the big clubs came in including Celtic, Rangers and Manchester United.

A local Leeds United scout had also shown interest a year before anyone else did. I'd visited Leeds and met Don Revie. He seemed very sincere and had a game plan about what he wanted to do. I settled on signing for Leeds and was due to return on the Tuesday after my final game for Scotland Schoolboys, against England Schoolboys at Ibrox, as I was leaving school.

Don and Leeds chairman Harry Reynolds were at the game. I scored twice in a 4-3 win. Following the game, Manchester United put a lot of pressure on my family and I arranged a meeting with them on the Tuesday morning, but rang Don to let him know. Don drove up with Harry Reynolds on the Monday night, got a speeding ticket, but caught the last ferry across the Forth. They got to our home at midnight and I signed the relevant forms. After a couple of hours' sleep, we drove back to Leeds. When Manchester United arrived, I was long gone.

It was a decision that people questioned because, after all, Manchester United was Manchester United, but there was something happening at Leeds United. There were many young players down at the club like Billy Bremner, Norman Hunter, Paul Reaney, Terry Cooper and Gary Sprake. Don was very convincing. He said, these are smashing players and we are going to be the team of the future. It was a bit of a pipe dream, but the way he said it, you believed him.

My parents were happy that Don would look after me, but it was still a difficult period as I settled in. I was not homesick as such, but I didn't enjoy being in lodgings with six other boys, no disrespect to Norman and Terry who were among the lads. In Dundee, I'd lived in a peaceful home with just my brother, so I did not enjoy having to fight for the bathroom and last cup of tea. I went home every six weeks. Making the return journey at first there were tears, but I soon realised that if I wanted to make it I had to be strong in mind and very strong in ambition.

Billy Bremner used to drop me off at the digs after training and asked me one day how I was enjoying it. I told him I liked being at Leeds, but didn't like the digs. Billy told me he was getting married, so I'd be on my own at his landlady, who was great, if I wanted. I got through the next couple of months and moved in. I quickly settled down.

I'd been at the club six months when I got my first team break aged 15. Billy had gone home to Scotland for a few days, but had not returned. Don called me out of the stands on the Friday and said, "Billy's not back; you're in the first team tomorrow." It was September 1962. Without being big-headed, I thought , "I'm ready for this, why did it take so long?"

I fully enjoyed playing in a home league game against Southampton with John Charles, Big Jack and Bobby Collins. Gary, Norman and Paul had just broken into the side as Don gave a number of the promising youngsters a chance. Mick Addy also got a first team opportunity that day, but would not feature again. It was a day when Big Jack broke his nose and had to go off. There were no substitutes, so John moved into defence and played his best game on his return to Leeds. I acquitted myself quite well. It was a big occasion for me. Following a 1-1 draw, I went back into the juniors and reserves, but I knew my chance would come again.

I played in a League Cup match at home to Swansea Town at the start of the 1963/64 season, but just when I was on the verge of breaking through I cracked a bone in my leg right after my 17th birthday playing in the youth cup at Sheffield Wednesday, which put me back a few months. It sapped my confidence, but, once fit, it was plain sailing.

I cemented a first team place during the 1965/66 season. I had come to Leeds with a reputation for scoring goals and began to show what I was capable of after getting my first goal for the club in a 3-2 defeat at Tottenham Hotspur. I ended the campaign as top scorer with 19 goals. Apart from getting a first senior hat-trick in the FA Cup against Bury, more significant were goals in the Fairs Cup against SC Leipzig, Valencia and Ujpest Doza as we reached the semi-finals.

The following season again we went close to success, losing in an FA Cup semi-final to Chelsea and Fairs Cup final against Dynamo Zagreb. The defeat to Chelsea left a bitter taste because of my last minute disallowed goal. The wall lined up, Peter Bonetti dived, the ball went in and everyone thought, "it's the equaliser," but that was not the case. Poor decisions by referees would be something we'd get used to.

Despite the disappointments, we were gaining experience. I knew we could win trophies and would not have to wait long. By New Year 1968, we were pushing for honours. Finally, we picked up our first major trophy when a Terry Cooper strike defeated Arsenal in the League Cup final at Wembley. The result was a significant step for us.

That campaign brought me 30 league and cup goals as I finished top scorer again. In the League Cup, I scored a hat-trick against Luton Town. In the Fairs Cup, I struck eight en route to the final, including four against Spora Luxembourg. The final against Ferencvaros was delayed until the 1968/69 campaign. We won with a goal by Mick Jones, who Don bought from Sheffield United for a club record fee to replace Alan Peacock. By the end of the season, we were First Division champions, which was a mega-thing.

Albeit we were doing really well and received plenty of praise, but the press, especially in London, loved putting us down and did so at every opportunity. The coming season was a massive one for us. We would be playing in the European Cup for the first time and looked forward to the challenge.

Don strengthened the side in attack and paid a British record fee for Allan Clarke during the close season. Allan's arrival and the departure of Mike O'Grady saw me move to the right wing. With Eddie, who also switched positions, and me on the flanks, combining with Allan and Mick in the middle, we had many options in attack. Our first team was a match for anyone and Don wanted to win every game and competition with the same 11 players. From 12

We became a team of household names. Whenever I meet not only Leeds supporters, but also fans of other sides from our era, they all know the great Leeds United team, Sprake, Reaney, Cooper, Bremner, Charlton, Hunter, Lorimer, Clarke, Jones, Giles, Gray and Madeley. I've always listed 12 players because Paul Madeley always played filling in for injuries and suspensions.

We had some real characters in our side. In his early days, Jack Charlton was a bit of a rebel and, no disrespect to the guys before us, when he began to play with top quality players he became a world class centre-back. Jack owed a great debt to Don because he got hold of him and made him play. Jack wanted to do things his way. Whereas Norman would win the ball and pass it to Billy or Johnny, Jack felt he could pass it as well as they could. We knew that was a joke, but you try telling Jack.

At one team meeting, Don said, "has anyone any points?" Pointing at Johnny, Jack said, "he keeps coming back and I have to give him the ball. Why can't he piss off up the field and I'll pass those balls?" Don said, "look Jack, Johnny is good at one thing, you're good at another. When Johnny comes off, give him the ball." Don put him in his place, but that was Jack, he genuinely thought that he could do it. If we'd had a weaker manager, Jack would have gone over the top on him. Don, like Alf Ramsey, was a strong character, so got the best out of him. Jack on his day was tremendous.

I'd started out my Leeds career playing alongside the main striker, which meant I was involved in the thick of the action. I made an impact. Now I was out wide, but me and Eddie were never really happy being out wide. We both preferred to get more involved, so went a little deeper into midfield. We weren't really out-and-out wide players, we dropped back and switched between 4-4-2 to a 4-2-4.

My game was different to Eddie's and we played to our strengths. His game was all about taking players on and dribbling past them whereas mine was more direct. If a cross was not on that was fine, my range of passing was good, I'd ping a ball over from distance to Mick or Allan at the back post. I always tried to release the ball quickly and played a simple game.

My shooting power was a great asset to have in my game. If I was not having the best of matches, a free-kick may come along and, bang, I'm the hero. Hotshot Lorimer scores again! Balls then were heavier than modern ones. When conditions were wet or muddy you could not make shots bend or dip like you can now, so power was crucial. I knew from a free-kick that a keeper would struggle to hold my shot, so would simply blast it. If he saved it Billy or Allan were ready to pounce on a rebound. We scored many goals from that tactic. Most of my open play goals came from outside or just inside the box. I'd pick up the ball from deep and when I got to around 40 yards out, I'd think to myself, have a crack. Many times, I'd hear one of the lads giving me stick for not passing, then bang, top corner. The stick stopped.

The arrival of Allan Clarke gave us something extra. Allan was so clinical in front of goal. With his finishing ability and Mick Jones' work-rate leading the line, they developed into a great partnership. Mick was such a hard worker and chased any lost cause. His unselfish running created openings.

Don was a fantastic manager, but he never really believed in his full squad. At the time, all the lads wanted to play, but when you look at the game nowadays, how teams prepare players for a season, top players know they will not play every game. Late on in a season we did, on occasion, run out of steam and in hindsight, without being too critical on Don, squad members could have come in against weaker sides. Don was very meticulous, but he did give too much respect to some teams, especially lower league sides in cup competitions. By the end of his team talk, you would have thought we were playing Real Madrid, but that was Don's way.

You cannot knock his record though. When you look at the trophies, then finals and semi-finals we reached, it was unbelievable. The commitment and will to win was tremendous, but at crucial times games caught up with us. Everyone remembers 1969/70 when we failed to win anything after coming so close on three fronts, but for me the campaign that stood out was 1971/72 when we beat Arsenal in the FA Cup final then had to play Wolves 48 hours later to clinch the double. Mick Jones was out, Allan Clarke, Johnny Giles and Eddie Gray were injured, but rather than use the squad,

Don picked them all. They battled, but there were fit lads on the sidelines that could have given more.

Sometimes losing can make you more bonded as a team. You look at the situation, the press would be having a dig, pre-season they'd say, "Leeds won't win anything." It gives you an inner strength as a team to show them. We were always able to battle back after a major defeat. That was one of our great strengths. Our cup final defeats to Sunderland and AC Milan inspired the championship campaign in 1973/74, no question.

By that second title, the great side had begun to break up as Gordon McQueen, Frank Gray, Terry Yorath and Joe Jordan replaced Big Jack, Terry and Mick. All went on to enjoy good careers internationally and at club level. During the 1974 close season, change was occurring. Suddenly Don had gone, Brian Clough was coming in and there was not the same desire and it showed domestically, but the players had one bone to pick, the European Cup.

Clough hated the Leeds set up. At the first team meeting he said we had not won anything fairly, we could throw our medals away and then he had a go at each player in turn. Not surprisingly, he only lasted 44 days before Jimmy Armfield took over. Things calmed down, but we were off the pace in the league and out of the League Cup. We had a decent FA Cup run before going out in the quarter-finals. The season was all about the European Cup.

Passionate and fanatical crowds could not intimidate us anymore. If opponents wanted to play, we could match them, but if they wanted a battle, we could do that as well. We knew the gamesmanship stunts foreign teams would pull. When under pressure, a player would go down injured to quieten the crowd. It was the same with throw-ins and free-kicks. We had seen it all before.

We had been the most consistent English team in Europe for a decade since making our European bow against Torino in 1965. Celtic and Manchester United had won the European Cup, Chelsea, Manchester City and Rangers the Cup Winners' Cup, while Newcastle United, Arsenal, Tottenham and Liverpool had claimed the UEFA Cup, formally the Fairs Cup. Only Celtic had reached two European finals, we'd been in four.

I'd played against Torino and experienced all our highs and lows in pursuit of European glory. We'd overcome Valencia, Bologna, Napoli, Ferencvaros, Standard Liege, Vitoria Setubal, Ujpest Dozsa, Dinamo Dresden, Juventus and Liverpool at the height of their powers. We'd had crunching wins against minnows like Spora Luxembourg and Lyn Oslo, suffered a shock defeat to SK Lierse and lost to great sides such as Real Zaragoza, Dinamo Zagreb, Celtic and Barcelona. We'd also won ties against Bologna and Napoli on the toss of a coin and lost out to AC Milan by virtue of scandalous refereeing.

Maurice Lindley was in charge as caretaker-manager when we started our European Cup campaign against FC Zurich. I slotted home a penalty in a 4-1 home leg win, before we saw out the tie comfortably. Jimmy Armfield was at the helm when we faced a tough trip to Ujpest Dosza in the second round. I gave us the edge with an early goal before we conceded a penalty. Big Gordon regained the advantage for us and we wrapped up the tie 3-0 win at home.

Anderlecht were dangerous opponents at a fog-bound Elland Road. David Stewart made his European debut with David Harvey out for the season following a car crash. I was doubtful myself, but managed to grab our third goal in the last minute to put us in great shape. We were never going to let a 3-0 lead slip. The match at Anderlecht was also affected by the weather, this time non-stop rain, but we won with a great strike by Billy.

In the semi-finals, we faced Barcelona, who had a tremendous history, but had not won the European Cup. They were a different proposition to our other opponents as they had big name stars including Dutch internationals Johann Cruyff and Johann Neeskens. The Spanish giants had built their side around Cruyff, a three-time European Cup winner with Ajax and a three-time European Footballer the Year award winner.

I didn't play in the home leg. I don't know why because I had the best scoring record for the club in Europe, but Jimmy had a knack of picking teams to stop opponents winning. In front of a 50,000 crowd, we won 2-1 with goals from Billy and Allan, but we should have gone out with more attacking options to bury them.

Jimmy realised that we had to get goals in the return leg because our lead would probably not be enough. If Barcelona won 1-0, we'd go out on away goals. Jimmy picked a more adventurous team, including three strikers in Joe, Allan and myself. Before the game, the lads' attitude was we wanted to win it for the gaffer and ourselves.

We were big stage players and psyched up. When you play football at that level, this is what it was all about and we had a knack of pulling off great away results in Europe. We expected to get through, although most pundits did not give us a chance.

Barcelona went at us from the kick-off, attempting to wipe out our one-goal advantage. Heredia went close with a header, but we made the perfect start when, within ten minutes, I thumped home a flick-on by Joe Jordan from a long David Stewart clearance for my 30th goal in Europe, a British record at the time. It was my most significant.

The goal knocked Barcelona back because they now needed to score three to win. In our minds, there was no way they would score three goals past us. Slowly though, they did pick up the pace and had a lot of possession, but with Big Gordon dominant in the air, little troubled our defence throughout the remainder of the half.

Barcelona regrouped during the interval. Their coach Rinus Michel brought on Rife and moved Marinho forward. Barcelona tore into us. Joe Jordan required stitches following a challenge, while Neeskens made his presence felt. It was getting physical, which was OK by us. As we battled away, Gallego received a booking for a challenge on Billy.

The home fans got progressively louder, sensing their team was coming back into the game. Barcelona were controlling midfield with Cruyff at the centre of everything, but we held firm. Norman was having an outstanding game; he was immense in the centre of defence.

We were not creating much as an attacking force, but kept battling away. Twenty minutes from time, Barcelona scored when Manuel Clares headed in a free-kick by Gallego. We had to stay calm, but within a few minutes, we put ourselves under enormous pressure when Big Gordon got himself sent off, retaliating with a punch when Clares pulled his shirt.

It was a stupid reaction by Gordon. He was in his first full season of European football and we'd warned him to keep his composure. We now had to dig deep, but I felt confident we could hold on. Paul Madeley, the original utility man, moved back from midfield following Gordon's dismissal to partner Norman. The final minutes were frantic as Barcelona pushed forward at every opportunity. David Stewart was not a flash keeper, but he was sound and proved to be a real hero as he kept Barcelona at bay with some terrific saves.

In the dying stages he kept out a Heredia header, then pulled off a sensational stop to deny a deflected shot by Cruyff, but he saved his best until last, when Neeskens gave Cruyff a chance in the last seconds, diving bravely at Cruyff's feet to secure a draw and an aggregate 3-2 victory. The celebrations afterwards were fantastic and the result was the highlight for me playing in Europe because it finally gave us a chance to win the European Cup.

Over 30 years on from our final defeat to Bayern Munich, I still have a sour taste about the way we lost. The penalty decision – or lack of it – when Franz Beckenbaur brought Allan Clarke down, was diabolical. Were it anyone other than Beckenbaur, who was famed for getting on at a referee, it would have been given. Sepp Maier then made a great stop from Billy with the score still 0-0. As for my 'goal', I had so many disallowed in my career, I always looked at the referee immediately. He pointed for a goal, but Beckenbaur ran over to the linesman and created a situation. You could see their goalkeeper and other players had accepted they were 1-0 down. There was no claim for offside. Beckenbaur made the big issue and his power won the day. Of course, Bayern went on to win with late goals from Roth and Müller. It was gut-wrenching..

Bad decisions by officials still decide more games than good play. You may be the best team, but lose out. Technology is available and should be used. It was sickening at the time, but all these years later, it has not taken away the euphoria or importance of my goal at the Nou Camp that got us through to the European Cup final.

When I look back at my career, I played at the highest level in internationals, World Cups and Cup finals, but for me the greatest thing was being a part of what Leeds United experienced at that time. For 10 years, we worked very hard and experienced highs and lows, but my main memory is not about winning or losing titles and finals, it was being part of something special.

We stayed at the top for a decade and was a winning team. Every year we made decent bonuses because we were challenging, but it was not about money. To wake up on a morning, get to the ground and enjoy the craic was fantastic. The spirit was amazing in the dressing room. It was full of laughter and happiness.

Even in the bad times, we enjoyed every minute. We played through injuries, but that is how it was. When I talk with the lads now, I have nothing but respect for them all and that is general from the group. We all got on; we didn't all go out with each other all the time. We palled up in small groups, but we were never happier than when we were in each other's company. It was truly special.

BRENDAN ORMSBY
CENTRE-HALF 1985–1990

BORN   1st October 1960, Birmingham
SIGNED   March 1985 from Aston Villa; £65,000
LEEDS CAREER   57 games, 7 goals
LEFT   Free transfer to Doncaster Rovers, July 1990

Brendan was a hard working central defender for Leeds United during the club's wilderness years in the mid-80s. Well-built and a no-nonsense tackler, Brendan was appointed captain when Ian Snodin joined Everton in January 1987. To supporters' surprise Billy Bremner's team went on a remarkable run that in 1986/87 saw them reach the FA Cup semi-final and Division Two promotion play-off final, rekindling supporter's faith. Brendan was a key player throughout the campaign, playing 43 matches with a never-say-die attitude. A bad knee injury in the play-off final ultimately ended his career.

Leeds United 2 v Queen's Park Rangers 1

FA Cup Fifth Round
Saturday 21st February 1987

Elland Road
Attendance 31,324

Underdogs Leeds United cause an FA Cup shock by knocking out First Division Queens Park Rangers

Teams

	Managers	
Billy Bremner		Jim Smith
Mervyn Day	1	David Seaman
Neil Aspin	2	Warren Neill
Mickey Adams	3	Robbie James
David Rennie	4	Clive Walker
(Sub. John Buckley)		(Sub. Sammy Lee)
Jack Ashurst	5	Gary Chivers
Brendan Ormsby	6	Terry Fenwick
John Stiles	7	Martin Allen
John Sheridan	8	Mike Fillery
		(Sub. Gavin Maguire)
John Pearson	9	Gary Bannister
Ian Baird	10	John Byrne
Andy Ritchie	11	Wayne Fereday
Baird 18, Ormsby 85	**Scorers**	Rennie (og) 64

Referee: K Barratt

WHEN BILLY BREMNER asked me to sign for Leeds United, I had no hesitation. When he asked me to be captain halfway through the 1986/87 campaign, I was honoured. It would prove to be an epic season, which would go down to the last kick. My highlight? That's easy, the euphoria in our dressing room after defeating Queen's Park Rangers in a FA Cup fifth round tie. It sparked a terrific run that only ended at the semi-final stage before we lost out in the Division Two play-off final. We ultimately failed, but went down fighting.

Two of my eight brothers, I am the youngest of 13, were good footballers. Tommy was better than I was and if he'd put his mind to it could have been a professional footballer. I had a different attitude and played at every opportunity with lads who were two or three years older. It toughened me up and things just developed. I was determined to make it, represented my local school then district, and signed for Aston Villa as an apprentice.

I also captained England Schoolboys at Wembley Stadium, which was a tremendous experience. We went down the day before to get used to the surroundings. I loved the old stadium. They took us into the massive changing rooms, then we walked up the tunnel and out onto the pitch, which was amazing, even though no-one was there. I'd heard so much about Wembley, seen Cup finals and England games on television, so to play there for me was a dream come true. Around 60,000 came and we defeated Wales 4-1. From that game Clive Allen and Kevin Ratcliffe went on to win full international caps and be stars in the top flight.

Only a few members of either team made the step up from schoolboy to professional football. You needed talent, but also luck. Being in the right place at the right time is important. It's also significant who is in charge of the national team at the time. When I got the opportunity to join Aston Villa, I represented the England youth team, but also applied to play for the Republic of Ireland because I was qualified to do so. In those days, you could not switch to another country when you had played for a youth side. The rules have now changed, which for me was unfortunate because I would have loved the opportunity to compete at the highest level and would have had more chance with the Republic than England.

Before I signed professional I made my first team debut against Arsenal at Villa Park. We won 5-1. It was so different from reserve team football, especially stepping onto the park alongside Denis Mortimer and John Gidman and facing the likes of Liam Brady, Pat Jennings and Frank Stapleton. These were players I had only seen on television and read about, I had to pinch myself. Then playing at Anfield and seeing 11 red shirts including the likes of Dalglish, Souness, Hansen and Rush line up was unnerving at a young age, but you soon find out if you could cut it as a professional.

I was on the fringes of the first team when I snapped my ankle going into a block tackle at Villa Park. I missed the whole of the 1980/81 championship season, which was a major disappointment as the club won the League Championship, but I came back and played three games as Villa made it to the European Cup final. Against Bayern Munich, I was a member of the squad, but 17th man, which was another major blow, especially when two players on the bench had not played in earlier rounds. I was at the game, was part of the civic celebrations and am on the team picture, which is something to look back on, but I did not feel part of it.

I eventually forced my way into the side in place of Ken McNaught when he was injured, but got sent off for punching John Richards of Wolves in my fourth game because he kept elbowing me throughout the match. I thought he'd broken my nose when I threw the punch. I did not knock him out ,but I put him on the ground.

I got hate mail from Wolves fans after that and lost my place. Ken came back into the side, so I told Villa that I'd leave if I didn't play. I just wanted to play football, but manager Ron Saunders said I was tired. I wasn't tired, I was a young lad and could play three games a week. I went back into the reserves, but plugged away. Eventually I got back into the side and Ken joined West Brom. I played around three years on and off in the first team, which had started to break up since the European Cup win. Some fans thought it was broken up too quickly.

Mervyn Day by now was at the club and we got on really well. When Mervyn joined Leeds, we kept in touch and in 1985 he contacted me to tell me that Billy Bremner was thinking about signing me. I was interested. Mervyn told me that Billy was going to watch me in the reserves, which I'd rather he didn't do because there was more pressure on me to play well. Anyway, Mervyn kept ringing me and said they were interested, then Leeds signed David Rennie, who also played centre-half. I thought that was the end of my chances.

Mervyn assured me that Leeds wanted us both and eventually I got permission to speak to Billy about a transfer. I stopped at Mervyn's for a couple of nights, spoke to Billy and had no hesitation in joining Leeds, who were then in the Second Division. Some people felt I was taking a backward step leaving Aston Villa because I was dropping down a division, but I did not see it that way. Even though Villa was in the First Division, Leeds was a club with great tradition behind them. It was either stay in the reserves at Villa and pick up decent money or move on and make a name for myself. It was not a difficult decision.

Leeds United had great potential. They also had Billy as manager and if Billy Bremner thought I was good enough to sign for him there was no way I was going to change my mind. I came up in the February when there was snow on the ground and no games. Billy sent the first team to Old Trafford to play Manchester United Reserves just to give us a game.

Shortly afterwards, I made my debut against Huddersfield Town and scored, which was tremendous. There were only around 15,000 at Elland Road, but that did not matter to me. It was just great to be playing first team football again. To cap a great day we won. Afterwards a few of us went out to a pub in Bramhope and had a meal to celebrate. It felt great.

I partnered David Rennie in central defence. David was staying at a hotel, while I was at Mervyn's, so we went out a few times and are still great mates 20 years on. We had the basis of a good team with the likes of Meryyn, David, Andy Ritchie, Ian Snodin, John Sheridan, Neil Aspin and Ian Baird, but there was a clique of players and Billy wanted to break it up. We eventually finished the campaign mid-table.

Over the summer of 1986, Billy brought in Peter Haddock and John Stiles to strengthen the squad and when the season started, our aim was to win promotion. The club had experienced a number of poor seasons since being relegated, but could rely on good support if the good times came back. We were determined to have a real go, but I missed the opening game through injury.

Billy was a great boss and I loved playing for him. A few weeks into the season, we had a home game against Hull City coming up. I told Billy that I was struggling, so had an injection and had my ankle strapped up. I looked like an American footballer the way I was padded up. Billy said to me, 'I'd rather have you out there with one leg that someone else out there with two.' He knew that I would never pull out of anything and would do my best for him. We beat Hull 3-0 and I scored our third goal. I only missed four more games all season.

We made a reasonable start and kept in the pack for the play-offs. We had a steady team and with results, confidence grew. Elland Road started to become a fortress, but we suffered a terrible run over Christmas, which knocked us back. Thankfully I missed a 7-2 thumping at Stoke City. We were a tight group, though, and were determined to battle away.

Before the FA Cup third round, Ian Snodin joined Everton for big money. Snod's departure helped us because everything centred on him. Snod was captain and our star player, but when he left, we became more of a team. It was a bit like what happened to Everton when they sold Wayne Rooney. Billy boosted the squad by bringing in John Pearson, Micky Adams, Bobby McDonald and Mark Aizlewood.

Billy made me captain. He was a great player and captain himself, so it was a massive honour. I'd captained England Schoolboys, England Youth and now Leeds United, which was fantastic and 20 years on, I'm honoured to have led the team. There have been better players and better captains at Leeds United than me, but whenever I go to a sports forum or club function I am introduced as Brendan Orsmby 'Former Leeds United Captain'. That means an awful lot to me.

I got on great with Billy. They say a team has 11 captains, but there is only one with the armband. Billy used to tell me things that he wanted to get across on the pitch. Off the pitch, I liaised with the players. If anyone had an issue, I spoke to the gaffer and I went back to them. I enjoyed the responsibility.

Billy was an inspirational manager, but on occasion, he was not the best tactician. Some teams Billy picked could not play the formation he wanted. At one point, we played three centre-backs, David Rennie, Jack Ashurst and myself. David was not bad on the ball, but Jack and I were typical centre-halves. We could get it down and play it now and again, but we were not a Lawrenson, Hansen or Ferdinand. Billy wanted us to play it from the back, but it did not work. We did not possess players for that system. Nevertheless, Billy always wanted to try different things.

In the FA Cup third round, we drew Telford United away. It was always a welcome distraction playing in the FA Cup and like all sides, we hoped for a good run. It was not going to be an easy match and with our league form looking a bit shaky at the time, we needed a boost. The last thing we needed was to get knocked out by a non-league side, so we went into the game determined to stamp our authority on the match.

It was one of those banana skin games when Telford had everything to gain and we had everything to lose. We were expected to win, but conditions made it favourable for them. In freezing weather, our official team coach broke down on the way to West Brom's ground (Police had moved the match), so we turned up in an old one. When we arrived, club officials would not let us in as they thought we were not Leeds United. Eventually we got in. The pitch was rock hard, but we got the result. Ian Baird scored twice and we came away with a 2-1 win.

Next up was another tricky tie, away to Swindon Town. Again, we were expected to win, but it was going to be a tough encounter, so we had to be focussed and had a job to do. We did, and came away with another hard-fought 2-1 victory. Ian scored the winner. Our confidence was growing by the round.

On the Monday, after training, we listened to the fifth round draw in the players lounge on the radio. Out of the hat came Queen's Park Rangers of the First Division at Elland Road. We were slightly disappointed as Rangers were not a bad team, but they were struggling in the league. However, at home we felt confident that we'd cause them problems. Our league form was improving, but for supporters, it was all about the FA Cup.

The build up was great. The biggest crowd for years was expected, it would be the largest and most passionate attendance we'd played in front of at Leeds. The anticipation was enormous because a place in the quarter-finals was at stake.

Billy began his pre-match routine in the same way after training on the Friday. We always finished with a five-a-side game and Billy would then have a little chat with us all, telling us to watch ourselves and prepare properly for the game. There was added spice to his words this time with the importance and profile of the game

When we arrived at Elland Road for pre-match, you could sense more supporters were milling around. The tension was obvious and there was real excitement in the air. We went through our normal preparation, but this was different, this was a big game. We had a team talk, then another one in the dressing room. It was mainly Billy talking, but a number of players had a few words to gee up the lads. I always geed them up. That wasn't just because I was captain, It was more because I could not play football and keep my mouth shut. I was vocal on and off the pitch.

Pre-match is so important for a player. The lads went through individual rituals, but there were more nerves than usual in the dressing room, you could sense it. It was important to have a quiet word with some of the lads. I always got nervous before matches; I still do even for a charity match. That was my nature. If I was not nervous, I'd be concerned. Being nervous

The first match against Bolton was a tough encounter, but in the replay, we played some wonderful football and eventually triumphed 3-2

Major Frank Buckley was a real character and an inspirational manager

John Charles (left) and Jim McCabe were part of our formidable half-back line which helped us defeat Bolton

A policeman uses a 'new-fangled' walkie-talkie during the quarter-final at Highbury, which we were unlucky to lose 1-0

Bobby Collins was an inspiration to all the young lads trying to make the grade at Elland Road in the early 60s

After a very tight and dour first game, we knew the replay would be a tense affair

Gary Sprake saves from Manchester's 1963 FA Cup final goalscoring hero David Herd early in the replay

Billy Bremner comes up trumps, acrobatically turning the
ball home for our late, late winner…

…and then is hurled into orbit by Jim Storrie in celebration of reaching
Wembley for the first time in the club's history

TERRY COOPER – 1968
ARSENAL 0 v LEEDS UNITED 1

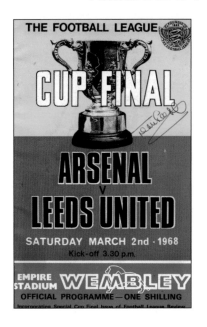

Having lost the 1965 FA Cup Final, we were determined to win on our next visit to Wembley

The Leeds fans turned out in force to support us at the Twin Towers

A moment I'll never forget as the ball fell to me to volley past Arsenal goalkeeper Jim Furnell

Don Revie celebrates at the final whistle with trainer Les Cocker

Ferencvaros keeper Istvan Geczi collects the ball under pressure from Bremner (no. 4) and Mick Jones in the home leg

Mick Jones forces the ball home for the only goal of the two-legged final

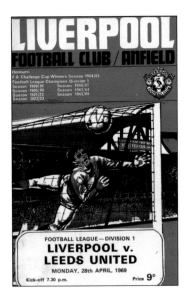

Eddie Gray takes on Ian Callaghan (no.7) and Chris Lawler
on a rare foray forward as we smothered Liverpool to lift
the first League title in the club's history

The celebrations were
unforgettable in our dressing
room after the game

Captain Billy Bremner and keeper
Gary Sprake show off the trophy after
our final home game of the season
against Nottingham Forest

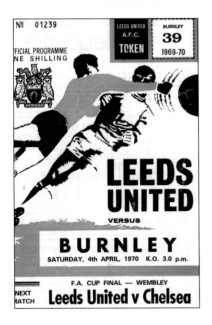

The goals I scored against Burnley in the last game before the 1970 FA
Cup Final were probably the best I ever scored

The 1969/70 team with me back row fourth from left,
standing next to Allan Clarke (fifth left)

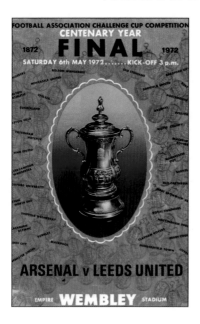

Our fans were incredible as they took over London for the day and lifted us to win the big one…The Centenary FA Cup final

My diving header is on its way into the net past the diving reserve goal-keeper Geoff Barnett and Arsenal's No.6, Peter Simpson. It fitted perfectly!

There's nothing like lifting the FA Cup up to a horde of adoring fans at the Twin Towers

I felt so sorry for Jonah (Mick Jones), who had to be helped up the steps to collect his medal after dislocating his left elbow at the end of the game

Barcelona were formidable opponents. Captain and Dutch maestro
Johann Cruyff is crouching second from left, with countryman
Johan Neeskens front row extreme right

Billy Bremner wheels away after scoring a vital goal to give us a
2-1 first leg platform, which we built on thanks to my goal at the
Camp Nou to give us a 1-1 draw there and a 3-2 overall victory.
We were at last through to our first European Cup Final

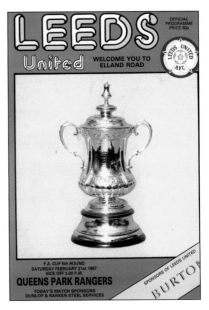

My favourite match of my Leeds career was the day we beat First Division QPR 2-1 and I scored the winning goal with five minutes to go!

Manager Billy Bremner celebrates my late winning goal

From the moment I joined Leeds I had a superb relationship with the fans and loved every minute of it, scoring some memorable goals. But the crowning moment for me was the win at Bournemouth which clinched promotion back to the to flight

Gordon Strachan was a huge influence on our push for promotion

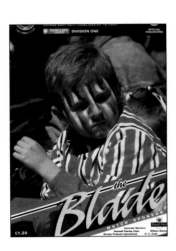

I was right on the spot to congratulate Jon Newsome on scoring the goal that put us 2-1 ahead. I thought we had it won then, but…

…it wasn't until the bizarre own goal scored by Sheffield's Brian Gayle that we really knew we had just about got our hands on the League title

Howard Wilkinson and Chairman Bill Fotherby celebrate with the trophy before our last game at home to Norwich City

I always loved playing against Manchester United and here I swoop to beat Gary Pallister to the ball to head home the winner in my favourite game...

...and celebrate behind the goal with the fans, Harry Kewell and Rod Wallace

There's not a lot to beat the feeling of having just seen off Fergie's men

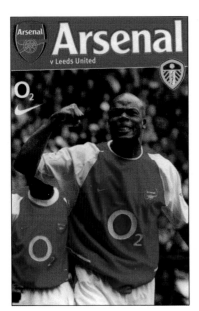

Ian Harte's free-kick has just put us 2-1 ahead against
the title-chasing Gunners

Mark Viduka lashes in the
late winner…

…to spark huge celebrations
amongst the Jimmy Saville fans
who had travelled to see us stay up

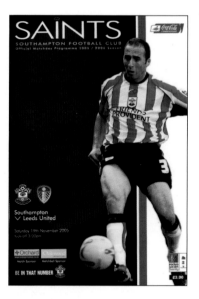

Playing for Leeds means playing with pride and passion…and that's what we came up with during that incredible second half at Southampton

Saluting those incredible fans after the win at St. Mary's

helped me focus on a game and this was a big one. Everyone had certain routines and some players were more superstitious than other were. I always wanted to be ready early so I was not rushing towards the end.

Inside the stadium when we ran out, the noise level was much higher than normal. The hairs stood up on the back of my neck. The bigger the game was, the bigger the crowd and the bigger the prize, the bigger supporters' anticipation. You could sense that as we ran out. The noise from home fans was incredible.

We were pumped up and got into Rangers' players from the kick-off. It was so important to let them know they would be in for a battle. They had silky skills, but we would run non-stop. Big John Pearson was looking for his first goal since his arrival at Leeds, but he offered us more than just goals with his height. John caused problems whenever we launched the ball forward and was involved when we deservedly opened the scoring on 18 minutes.

Micky Adams, another mid-season signing, was not letting winger Wayne Fereday get any freedom and whenever we went forward was looking to support the attack. From one such run he put in a perfect cross, Big John headed the ball back across the face of the goal for Ian to beat Gary Chivers to the ball and head beyond keeper David Seaman. It was a typical goal for Ian. He was such a brave player.

It was the perfect start for us as it meant Rangers could not sit back. They would have to come forward and attack us, which would create space. We knew that Rangers would not wilt, though, and they did force us back for a period. They had a good chance to equalise from a corner when we were slack with our marking, but Chivers put the ball wide, fortunately for us.

At half-time, Billy told us to keep it tight, but to keep pressurising them. It was important to try and get the second goal because we looked the more dangerous side. For spectators it must have been an exciting game to watch, as both sides were not holding back.

As in the first half, we nearly conceded through poor marking, but were delighted when Mervyn pulled off a brilliant stop to deny John Byrne on the hour. Mervyn, though, was powerless to prevent an equaliser a few minutes later when David Rennie, who had been so assured all afternoon, scored an own goal, but he was unlucky. David swung a leg at a cross and it hooked into the net. It was a blow, but we were not going to let all our hard work come to nothing.

I urged the lads for more effort. We had to raise our game, but as the minutes slipped by, it looked as if it the match may end in a draw and a replay on Rangers' dreaded plastic pitch. We didn't want that as it was a huge advantage to them. It was like playing on a car park floor.

We pushed forward again and again. Andy Ritchie went close from a tight angle and then with five minutes remaining, he forced a corner kick, which would signal my moment of glory. A straightforward centre by Shez [John Sheridan], who had been relatively quiet by his high standards, came over. It was a move straight from the training ground. Big John flicked the ball on at the near post. I got on the end of it at the far post to head powerfully past Seaman and three men covering on the goal-line. The keeper never had a chance. The ball flew in and my natural run carried me towards the Kop.

When I saw the ball enter the net, I totally lost it and jumped up on the fence to celebrate. The Kop also lost it in wild celebrations. I felt pure relief and elation mixed together and went mental. It was a good job the fence was there or I'd have been in with the supporters. As I was hanging up on the fence celebrating with the lads, I noticed a policeman walking towards us. I told the lads it might be better if we got down!

With so little time left, I hoped that would be it and luckily it turned out that way. For Leeds supporters, they'd had little to cheer in recent seasons, so I was really delighted for them and they celebrated. It had been a hard game; we'd done well and could be proud of ourselves.

Back in the dressing room, it was unbelievable. We'd had a great day and knew it would be a great night before getting back to the business of playing again. We made the most of the day; it was brilliant. For me it was also a great moment as, apart from scoring the winner, it was the first time I'd been in a team that had reached the last eight of the competition. The win sparked a purple patch for us and an amazing few months of highs and lows.

Come the Monday, we wanted to draw Wigan in the quarter-finals, as they were the weakest side left in the competition. We got our wish. Everyone was elated. Okay, it would be tough as it was away from home, but we were favourites to progress to the semi-finals. We thought we were just one game from Wembley.

I was suspended for the Wigan match, so had my fingers crossed that the lads would get through. I was confident they would as we had enough experience in the squad to make it. I covered the match on local radio. We won it quite comfortably. Once John Stiles scored, Wigan had to come at us and we got a second through Micky Adams to seal victory. Apart from Mervyn, who won an FA Cup winners medal with West Ham in his early days, this was a new experience for us all. It was an exciting time.

We were now in the semi-finals of the FA Cup. Coventry City were our next opponents, which was not too bad. We'd have preferred Watford, but it was not to be. We certainly did not want Spurs, who were favourites. It was not going to be easy as they had been on a good run themselves and had beaten Manchester United at Old Trafford.

The build up was fantastic and brought the club a lot of media attention, which no-one would have predicted at the start of the season. Newspapers, radio and television was at the club every day before the match. We formed a players pool, but realised that money would only come pouring into the pool if we won the semi-final. That was for another day and would take care of itself; our focus was on Hillsborough with a noon kick-off.

We stayed over in Sheffield the night before. The hotel was buzzing and all the attention was on us as a squad. As a professional footballer, it was fantastic to be part of, but we knew it would be on a different scale for the final. But for now, this was the biggest game of our lives and we could have been 3-0 up at half time, but settled for David Rennie's header. Coventry had a lot of pressure in the second half and created a few chances. We were riding our luck.

It's nearly 20 years since the game and in all that time I've never tried to make an excuse for my mistake that brought Coventry their equaliser. A long ball went over my head and I was trying to shield it over the line, Dave Bennett hooked his foot around my legs. It was virtually over the line, but he kept it in by inches. My momentum took me running onto the track. Dave got up and crossed it across the face of the six-yard box for substitute Micky Gynn to stick it in off his shin. I should have whacked the ball straight out of play, no doubt.

Coventry then took the lead through Keith Houchen. Billy brought Keith Edwards on and, when he equalised, I ran the quickest 60 yards I've ever covered in my life. He'd saved my life.

Extra-time; and whoever scored first would win, unfortunately it was not to be for us as Bennett grabbed the winner. There were many tears in our dressing room, especially from me, and the journey back to Leeds was the worst I made after a football match. We were all so down, but had to pick ourselves up for the play-offs, although right then that was the furthest thing from our minds.

We had to play Shrewsbury Town in a league game on the Tuesday night. Billy took us down on the Monday just to get us away from Leeds and the depressing publicity in the aftermath of the semi-final. We'd played in front on 50,000, now it was 4,000 and chucking down with rain. We had to get the semi-final out of our system, so actually the match came at a great time. We did a professional job and won the game. We went on and I managed to grab a couple of winning goals against Ipswich Town and West Brom, which clinched a play-off place. The dressing room was buzzing again. We had a number of Mickey-takers amongst our number. John Sheridan was always in the middle of things, so was John Stiles.

It was actually the first season of the play-offs and they weren't quite the same format as we have today. As we finished fourth, we faced Oldham Athletic in the semi-final and avoided First Division Charlton Athletic, who were given a chance to avoid the drop by taking part. Oldham had been a bogey team for us, but in front of a packed house at Elland Road we won with a last minute winner from Keith Edwards, who always seemed to score those vital goals. In the return, they went 2-0 up with a minute of normal time remaining. We were going out. When the ball hit the back of the net for their second, my first thought was, "where we are going on holiday?" I could see no way back. Amazingly, we knocked the ball up and Keith stuck it in. We were ahead on away goals (which counted when the play-offs first started, unlike now) and held on in extra-time. The dressing room was delirious.

Against Charlton in the final, we lost the opening leg to a Jim Melrose goal late on, but levelled it up at Elland Road, when I scored, but it was not enough to win the tie overall. I was injured during the first half of the play-off replay, so watched from the sidelines and thought we'd done it when Shez scored late on with a brilliant free kick. When Peter Shirtliff equalised, I knew it would not be our night. Then Shirtliff scored another to win the game.

It was a bitter blow. For me, personally, I knew that I'd be out for a long time because I had a bad injury to my left knee. It was my own fault because, as I tried to take Garth Crooks out of the game, my knee twisted and I knew something had gone. I was out for 16 months. I had ruptured the cruciate ligament, ripped the medial ligament and displaced the medial cartilage. Today, I'd have got back quicker. I realised my time at Leeds was up. I played one more game before teaming up with Billy at Doncaster and then played briefly for Waterford, Wigan and Scarborough.

People often ask me whether I was more disappointed to lose in the FA Cup semi-final or play-off final. For me it was definitely the semi-final because we realised that we would probably never get that close again to the final of the biggest cup competition in the world, whereas the play-offs come around every year. Football-wise it was the biggest disappointment of my career. The competition has so much history; to take part in a showpiece final would have been brilliant. Some players however go through a career and never get to the semi-final, so I still take something from our run.

Playing is the best part of being a professional footballer, but that is linked to the banter, so when you finish playing that is the hardest thing to adjust to because every day its banter, banter, banter. It's brilliant; there are different characters in the dressing room. Some are quiet, others are at the centre of everything, but it all generates the team spirit you need to be successful. Everyday something is going on, someone is taking the Mickey out of each other and it is something you do miss because it is gone.

I see a number of the lads when I play in Masters football and when the ex-Leeds United team play it's as if we were playing 20 years ago. The banter and Mickey-taking starts all over again. We had tremendous team spirit and it was encouraged by the gaffer. Billy Bremner was a legend in football and is sadly missed. As a person, I loved listening to his stories. I heard them all at Leeds, but then wanted to hear them again at Doncaster Rovers when he was manager and took me there briefly. When Billy spoke, you sat and listened.

Billy had incredible enthusiasm, a tremendous attitude and loved all the lads. Billy came in every day to change with us in the dressing room, had a laugh and a joke with everyone, but when it came to work, the serious side of him took over. Billy was one of the best people I ever met in my life football-wise and as a man as well.

I loved my time at Leeds United and was lucky enough to enjoy four great years. I loved the great banter with the supporters and still do when I see them on match days. I was privileged to be captain and will never forget the ups and downs of the 1986/87 season. I only scored seven goals for Leeds, they were all important, but the one that February afternoon in the FA Cup against Queen's Park Rangers was the most memorable. The season ended in tears, but all these years on, I still recall the elation I felt when my header that day hit the back of the net. It will always stand out.

MEL STERLAND
RIGHT-BACK 1989–1994

BORN   1st October 1961, Sheffield
SIGNED   July 1989 from Rangers; £600,000
LEEDS CAREER   146 games, 20 goals
HONOURS   1 Division One Championship, 1 Division Two
Championship, 1 England cap, 7 England U21 caps
LEFT   Retired due to ankle injury, 1994

Mel was an immensely popular player for Leeds United during the club's renaissance in the 1990s. A swash-buckling attacking right-back, Mel, nicknamed 'Zico' by Leeds fans due to his booming shot, which brought him spectacular goals, made his name at Sheffield Wednesday before a brief spell at Rangers. A strong tackler, Mel created numerous goals with pinpoint crosses. Continually motivating players around him, Mel enjoyed a tremendous rapport with Leeds supporters. A crowd-pleaser, fans loved his gestures after a trademark goal.

Bournemouth 0 v Leeds United 1

Division Two
Saturday 5th May 1990

Dean Court
Attendance 9,918

*Leeds United claim victory in the final game of the season to clinch the
Second Division title*

Teams

Harry Redknapp	**Managers**	Howard Wilkinson
Gerry Peyton	1	Mervyn Day
Kevin Bond	2	Mel Sterland
David Coleman	3	Jim Beglin
Peter Shearer	4	Vinnie Jones
Paul Miller	5	Chris Fairclough
Gavin Peacock	6	Peter Haddock
(Sub. Richard Cadette)		
Sean O'Driscoll	7	Gordon Strachan
Shaun Brooks	8	Chris Kamara
Trevor Aylott	9	Lee Chapman
George Lawrence	10	Bobby Davison
		(Sub. Imre Varadi)
		(Sub. David Batty)
Luther Blissett	11	Gary Speed
	Scorers	Chapman 49

Referee: R Gifford

I JOINED LEEDS UNITED at an exciting time and was convinced that the club, with my former manager at Sheffield Wednesday, Howard Wilkinson, in charge, was about to go places. In my first season, the target was promotion. It was a hard campaign and we had to handle the pressure of being pre-season favourites. There were many memorable matches, but none more than our win in the last game at Bournemouth that clinched promotion and the championship. Two years on, we'd land the Division One title. It was an amazing few seasons, which started on a red-hot day on the south coast.

I was the youngest of nine children and grew up on a rough estate. I enjoyed playing football and represented my school, South Yorkshire and Sheffield Boys, which was fantastic. Then a scout at Sheffield Wednesday spotted me. I'd supported Wednesday since being a kid and used to watch them from the Kop, so it was tremendous to train at Hillsborough. My heroes were Roger Wylde and Chris Turner. I trained hard and got selected for the nursery team, Middleton Rovers. My parents travelled everywhere to see me play.

Sunderland and Lincoln City wanted to sign me as an apprentice, but there was only one club for me, Sheffield Wednesday. I got my wish and made my first team debut at 17 in a midweek fixture against Blackpool. I was substitute and came on for a few minutes. It was an unbelievable feeling, something I'll never forget. It was nowhere near a full house, but to me that did not matter at all. I was playing for my hometown club.

My mum saw me play, which meant a lot to me because she wasn't well and died before I made my full debut against Hull City on the Saturday. It was an emotional time, but I wanted to face Hull and do her justice for believing in me. We lost 2-1, but I scored and thought, "that's for you, mum." It was tough, but I had an opportunity and knew I must get on with making my mark.

Initially I played centre-forward, but manager Len Ashurst switched me to midfield. Although I'd broken into the first team, it wasn't happening for me. I was not enjoying my football and was unsure if I'd be offered professional terms, but then Jack Charlton took over as manager. Our chief scout suggested to Jack that I might do well at right-back. Jack initially refused because I'd never played in that position, but one day we were due to play Grimsby Town who had a really quick left-winger. Jack put me in and I never looked back. Jack stayed a couple of years before Howard Wilkinson became manager.

Under Howard, I played my best football for Wednesday. People used to criticise the long ball style, but it got results, which is what supporters want. We won promotion to Division One. We clinched our top-flight place at Cardiff City. At first, we thought we'd won the title until we heard that Chelsea had defeated Grimsby. It was disappointing, as we'd led the way during the season, but it was still superb to go up. I could not wait to play in Division One against the likes of Kenny Dalglish and Bryan Robson.

When I set out as an apprentice, I had two ambitions, to be a professional footballer and play for my country. I achieved both. Playing for England meant everything. I played for the U21s, the B-side and full team. When I played for the U21s, we won the European Championships, beating Spain in the two-legged final. I scored the only goal in Seville, before we won the home leg comfortably. Although I only won one full cap, versus Saudi Arabia under Bobby Robson, I felt incredibly proud.

Winning trophies to me was a major target, but you have to consider them a bonus and not expect to win. At Sheffield Wednesday, we reached the FA Cup semi-finals in successive years, losing to Brighton & Hove Albion and Everton. We were favourites to defeat Brighton, but didn't perform. You see players cry on television after major cup defeats. I've been there. Every footballer dreams of playing in a cup final, both defeats really hurt.

When Howard became Leeds United manager a few games into the 1988/89 campaign, Peter Eustace took over at Wednesday. I was sorry to see Howard go. There was speculation that Sunderland wanted to sign me. I was feeling unsettled, but before anything developed Peter got the sack. I was not happy, so put in a transfer request because there were rumours that Rangers wanted to sign me as well.

Wednesday appointed Ron Atkinson manager. I arranged a showdown meeting; big Ron was a real character. For whatever reason I had no socks on, which eagle-eyed Ron spotted. I explained my reasons for wanting to leave. I had a chance to play for a top side in Europe. Ron said, okay, but added, next time I come to his office, put socks on. His comment broke the ice. We had a laugh; opened some champagne and Ron wished me well.

Ron agreed it would be a great move for me and I duly signed for Rangers in an £850,000 deal. I was happy in Scotland, but only lasted a few months. I played in the Scottish Cup final when we lost to Celtic, but we did win the Scottish Premier League, finishing comfortably ahead of Aberdeen. During the summer, I was about to go on a family holiday to Spain when Ron Atkinson rang and offered me the chance to return to Wednesday. Then Trevor Francis at Queen's Park Rangers rang and asked me to join. I rang Rangers manager Graham Souness to find out what was happening. He told me he'd bought Trevor Steven, so had to balance the books. He was listening to offers for me.

I told Ron I'd think it over and agreed to speak to Trevor, when suddenly Howard Wilkinson rang. Howard said, "do you fancy coming to Leeds United? I'm building a squad to win the league." I said, "pardon?" Howard repeated himself, "do you fancy coming to Leeds United? I'm building a squad to win the league." I explained that I'd spoken to Sheffield Wednesday and had an option to return. Howard said, "you've served your time at Wednesday. You did well. Don't go back, it would be a mistake. Take on a new challenge."

I then told Howard that I'd agreed to speak to Queen's Park Rangers. Howard said, "speak to them, but on your way back north, come and have a chat with Bill Fotherby and me. I want you to sign for Leeds United. We have big plans. I'm fetching good players in and it's going to be exciting. I want you to be a part of it." I agreed to see him after Trevor before deciding.

As planned, I met Trevor Francis, but quickly realised that I didn't want to move to London. I then met Howard and made the decision to join Leeds immediately. I knew Howard, and realised it was the right move for me. I could have returned to Sheffield Wednesday, but Howard was right, I needed to make my mark somewhere else. It was the right move at the right time. I moved back to Sheffield to live, as I am Sheffield lad at heart. I knew Wednesday fans would give me stick, but I put them right, I joined Rangers before Leeds.

I respected Howard for his man-management skills, coaching abilities and motivational skills. Gordon Strachan was already at the club along with Chris Fairclough. Others players to join included Vinnie Jones, John McClelland and John Hendrie. With the experience at the club, we were installed as title favourites. We'd been in Division Two since 1982, so the target in 1989/90 was promotion, nothing less.

Pre-season was always hard at Sheffield Wednesday, so I knew it would be tough at Leeds. I prepared myself for a slog and as expected, training was really demanding. Howard made sure we were fit. Howard got the balls out and worked with the players more than at Wednesday, but at times all we seemed to do was run. The lads used to joke that the training shoes were due for a 100,000-mile service!

There was a lot of hype surrounding Leeds pre-season, but we were ready and fully keyed up when the opening game came around at Newcastle United. We hoped for a great start, but then got hammered 5-2. Micky Quinn got four goals. Without making excuses for the defeat, it takes time for new players to blend. It was disappointing, but we got going with a lucky win against Middlesbrough, when Gary Parkinson scored a last minute own goal.

We quickly moved up the table. Supporters could see things were happening and got behind us. I struck up a great rapport with the Leeds fans and was delighted to grab my first goal with a 25-yard strike in a 2-1 win over Oxford United. I had a reputation for scoring long-range goals. The Leeds fans were always encouraging me to have a go. To hear them chant "Zico, Zico" was really great. I'd made an impact. It's also not bad being compared to a Brazilian great like Zico! The fans were tremendous; if the team gave everything, they appreciated it.

By the return against Newcastle, we were settled and playing well. It was a tough game. I cracked two ribs, but didn't fully realise until later when I went to hospital. We won 1-0 and it was great to play a part in our goal. Gordon played a terrific ball to me, which I took on the chest before whipping the ball in for Ian Baird to score at the far post. The atmosphere was buzzing because we had produced the goods.

At Christmas, we were in the mix alongside Sheffield United. We had to face Sheffield at Bramall Lane over the festive period. A couple of days before the game I was in a pub in Sheffield and local fans as usual gave me stick. One guy said, "I bet you don't score against United." I asked him where he stood at the ground. He told me, "the right corner flag as you come out of the player's tunnel." I bet him a fiver.

I was determined to get a goal, not just because of this guy, but also as I'd got some stick in the local press over recent weeks that I should be scoring more goals. My chance came in the first half when we got a free-kick at the Kop end 35 yards out. I put the ball down and Gordon Strachan said, "big man, what are you doing?" I replied, "Gordon, I fancy it. I'm gonna hit it." Gordon said, "go on big man." So I took it and I caught the ball really well and it flew into the top corner. Their keeper had no chance.

Running off to celebrate, I realised we were kicking towards where the guy in the pub was standing. I thought, "I'm gonna find that guy," so raced to the corner flag and bent the stick over. The guy gave me plenty of abuse, but I was not bothered because I'd scored a belter and taken a fiver off him. For some reason, I always seemed to score against Sheffield United. I have no idea why, but it naturally gave me a lot of pleasure!

The hard work was paying off and with the likes of Gordon Strachan in the team; there was quality around and it rubbed off on all the players. Gordon was top class. He is the best footballer I have worked with on and off the field. Gordon spoke his mind if you were not doing it on the pitch and let you know off the pitch if you were not pulling your weight. Gordon was so determined for us to succeed.

The young apprentices loved it and worked with Gordon to get tips. When we went out, Gordon made sure we all went, including our wives. Team spirit was superb. If we got beat on a Saturday, we worked on things on the Monday. Training was always interesting. We did lots of five and six-a-sides, worked on dead ball situations, especially free-kicks.

Some of us were surprised when Howard signed Vinnie Jones. He had a reputation for being a hard player, but Vinnie was as soft as a brush and very funny. Vinnie also did a lot of charity work, but because of his reputation when we went out everyone wanted to fight him. I remember one night at a nightclub some guy fancied his chances and began to wind Vinnie up. Vinnie said, "go away." This guy followed him into the toilet, so I went along because I knew something would happen. When I arrived, the guy was on the floor, he'd taken a pop at Vinnie. I asked what happened, Vinnie looked at me and said, "I warned him." Vinnie was great company, but also proved to be more than a hard player. He scored some great goals, one against Brighton was memorable and another strike against Hull City was particularly sweet.

David Batty had come through the ranks at Leeds. David used to whack balls all over the place in training during shooting practice. Gordon used to look at me and then stare up at the heavens. Batts was never going to be a prolific scorer, but he added bite in midfield. Gary Speed also broke through; he had pace and could score from midfield as he's proved throughout his long career. With Mervyn Day in goal, we had an experienced keeper, Chris Fairclough was a great lad and a terrific defender, but the player that stuck out for me was Peter Haddock. Peter could play anywhere, right-back, left-back, centre half, midfield. He was a great asset to the side.

There were plenty of jokers around, which developed a terrific dressing room spirit. Howard knew the characters he wanted, but playing for Leeds United there was an expectancy and pressure in every game. We revelled in it. Everyone was focused on getting promotion. With our team spirit, everyone just got on with it. Not one player in the squad said we were going to win the league, do this or do that. We got on with games week in and week out.

Early in the New Year, Lee Chapman arrived. Lee had a proven track record and added a cutting edge to our attack. Ian Baird was gutted and decided to leave, Bairdy worked hard, but wasn't a natural finisher like Lee. Howard was shrewd and it proved to be a great signing. Chappy would put his head in anywhere in the box. Okay, he wasn't brilliant on the deck, but Lee was brave and got on the end of balls.

We carried on picking up points, playing great stuff, but we could also battle. At Oxford United, we recovered from 2-0 down to win 4-2. It was a great victory and sent out a message that we would grind away. We won three on the spin against West Ham, Sunderland and Portsmouth, then experienced a dip in form that started with a defeat at Wolves. It was hard to put your finger on it, we just had to keep battling away and Wilko was superb. He told us to keep believing and stick together.

We didn't change our preparation, we kept believing and eventually hit back when we hammered Sheffield United 4-0. It was a massive local derby. Sheffield had been on fire alongside us in the promotion race, but we thumped them. Gordon scored a couple, while Gary Speed struck a great goal. It was buzzing inside Elland Road.

With three games remaining, the title was within reach, but we lost at home to Barnsley in a midweek match after taking the lead through a Chris Fairclough header. There was no time to mope around though as we faced Leicester City in our final home game of the season. It was a must-win game and the atmosphere inside Elland Road was electric.

I was marking my brother-in-law Tony James. Before the game, I was winding Tony up and told him that I'd get a goal. He told me I would not get a kick. The game was only a few minutes old when an opportunity came my way and I was not going to miss. Gordon rolled a ball inside to me as I was on the overlap. I raced to just outside the 18-yard box. I thought, "take another touch and whack it." I did, just as Tony came across my shot. The ball went through his legs and past keeper Martin Hodge into the bottom corner. The noise inside Elland Road was incredible as I wheeled away in delight. I have a picture at home just as I've hit the ball. The look on Tony's face is terrific. He's not happy!

In the second half, Leicester got back into the game through a great strike by Gary McAllister. It was a real blow. Gary almost added a second, but Mervyn pulled off a really fine stop. We knew a win was vital and kept battling away. Gordon kept urging us on and eventually we got the winner five minutes from time. Gordon controlled a ball on the edge of the penalty box before slotting in a dipping volley. The ball flew in. We went mental.

At the final whistle, there were great scenes of celebrations. For a moment, we thought we were up as a rumour went around that Sheffield United had not won, but that soon disappeared. It was all down to the final game at Bournemouth, who needed a win to stay up, while we needed a victory to clinch the title.

If we slipped up it was possible Sheffield United, level on points, but with an inferior goal difference, and Newcastle United, two points behind, could edge us out of automatic promotion. I was sure Sheffield would get a result against Leicester, but Newcastle had a tough task as Middlesbrough had to win to guarantee safety. A bizarre twist was that Ian Baird could do us a favour. Bairdy now played for Middlesbrough, if they won and we won; he'd claim a championship medal.

The build up during the week was very professional. Nobody was getting carried away with the excitement. We all knew our jobs. We knew that the club's destiny was in our hands. On match day, we had our team meeting around lunchtime when Howard gave his instructions. Back in Leeds, thousands prepared to watch the game on close-circuit feeds.

Travelling to the ground there were thousands of Leeds supporters partying on the beach, it was an unbelievable sight. The atmosphere was electric outside the ground and as we warmed up, there seemed to be Leeds fans everywhere, although only 2,000 were officially in the stadium. The temperature was scorching. This was the club's biggest game for years.

In the dressing room, we prepared in our own way. All the lads were psyched up. Howard knew who to put his arm around and who to gee up. I was nervous, but getting changed there was a good tension. I was geeing on the lads as usual; I'd always try and get the lads revved up. Gordon was offering words of encouragement and Vinnie was really fired up. Then as we lined up, final words of encouragement came from various players. "Come on, let's get at them, lets get among them, let's do it." The same team that faced Leicester City lined up at Bournemouth. We'd worked so hard, promotion depended on one game. At last, game on.

In the first half, we kicked towards our supporters massed behind one goal. Gary Speed tested the Bournemouth defence early on, before Chappy showed his aerial threat from a corner. We had a setback early on when Bobby Davison pulled up with a knee injury; he'd been doubtful during the week. Carl Shutt was a capable deputy and almost gave us the lead with a snapshot. Carl then went close again after being set up by Chappy from a great cross by Gary, but Bournemouth keeper Gerry Peyton made a terrific stop.

We'd made a positive opening and was creating havoc especially down the left flank. The lads had settled well. We had to be on our guard however and, after Lee went close, we had to react quickly to a counter-attack from Bournemouth. From a free-kick, Shaun Brooks curled a dangerous ball across our penalty box, which Jim Beglin was alert to and covered.

We were soon back on the attack and almost broke the deadlock when Chris Kamara had a shot deflected, which Peyton did very well to save. Bournemouth were not going to lie down and they created a marvellous opportunity to score when they had a three-against-one breakaway. It was a guilt-edged chance, but Peter Haddock snuffed out the opportunity with a brilliant last-ditch tackle on Luther Blissett. It was a real scare and illustrated that we could not lose our concentration for a split second.

Bournemouth felt lifted and forced us on to the defensive, but we soon re-established our authority on the game. I was just wide with a long-range effort before forcing Peyton into a save, but our clearest chance came in the dying seconds of the half when Bournemouth skipper Kevin Bond brought down our captain, Gordon Strachan. It looked a penalty but the referee disagreed.

The decision was a disappointment, but at half time, we were delighted to have a breather and took in fluids because it was red-hot. Howard told us to keep it tight, he was sure our experience would see us through. Sheffield United were already winning 4-2 at Leicester, while Middlesbrough were drawing 0-0 with Newcastle. As things stood, Sheffield United would be champions, while we sat in second place, but a lot of football was still to be played.

We had controlled the majority of the game and got off to a solid start again. Just after the resumption, we almost scored when Kevin Bond, under enormous pressure, sliced the ball against his own post. We were not to be denied, though, and struck the all-important opening goal on 49 minutes. I remember it as if it was yesterday. Chris Kamara made a great run down the right, before crossing a terrific ball for Chappy to plant a header into the bottom corner from six yards out. The keeper did not have a chance. We went mental. There was no way Bournemouth was going to deny us the title, no way.

Shortly after our goal, there was a massive roar from our supporters. Clearly, a result was going our way. Word came through that Middlesbrough had a 2-0 lead, then a 3-1 lead and Bairdy had struck one of the goals. Although Sheffield were winning, the title was in our grasp. One more goal would do it, but amazingly, neither side created an opening until the final moments when Chappy should have scored when clean through. But Lee's miss did not matter.

At the final whistle, there was massive relief and elation for the players and management team. We were also delighted for our fans, who invaded the pitch to celebrate. Sheffield United eventually won 5-2, while Newcastle went down 4-1 at Middlesbrough, but it did not matter, we were Division Two champions and it felt great. We were back in the big time.

In the dressing room afterwards it was fantastic. The chairman Leslie Silver came in, Bill Fotherby came in, there was a champagne everywhere. It was great. Howard, the coaching staff and all the lads were just so happy. It was a case of job done.

We all got legless on the coach home. We had scarves flying out the window, there was singing, chanting. It was a great journey home. Winning promotion as champions was a tremendous feeling. You never forget it. We played a friendly a few days later against Genoa where we got presented with the trophy. The atmosphere was just a big party.

My final seasons at Leeds were just as exciting because Howard was really determined to kick on. There was a feel good factor at the club in 1990/91. It was buzzing. Gary McAllister, Chris Whyte and John Lukic arrived. Crowds were up and it was a magic place to play football. We surprised teams and enjoyed some great victories, eventually finishing fourth in the league.

Pre-season, Rod Wallace and Tony Dorigo strengthened the squad. Some pundits tipped us as outsiders for the league. As a player, all you can do is play each game and see what develops. We made a great start, but it wasn't until the televised matches that journalists began to rate us. We won 4-1 at Aston Villa and played really well. I scored from a corner then set up one for Lee with a header. I played really well and thought, "I must get the man of the match award," but they gave it Lee. I could not believe it; I was gutted!

The 1991/92 campaign developed into a two-horse race between Manchester United and us. Over Christmas, Alex Ferguson's team knocked us out of both cups, but we got a draw at Elland Road in the league when I slotted in a penalty. Into the New Year and my first return to Sheffield Wednesday as a player came along. It was strange, but I was looking forward to it. I had a bit of a hamstring strain, but was determined to play and our 6-1 win in another televised match was an unbelievable result. It should have been 6-0 because their goal was never a penalty.

Lee got a hat-trick, Tony Dorigo also scored from a free kick. We practised the move in training and it worked a treat. I ran in as if to hit the ball, the ball was knocked to Gordon then Tony planted it into the top corner. That was a sweet moment. There was a friendly rivalry between Tony and me over who would score most goals. We had a laugh about it.

I'd scored two against Sheffield United earlier in the season during a bizarre 4-3 win after we'd been 4-0 up at half time. Gary and I had a chat over who would take a penalty that got us plenty of coverage in the papers. I'd been out injured, so Gary was due to take one, but I wasn't happy. We had a chat on the pitch. I won. There was pressure, but I tucked it away, which was a relief otherwise I'd have been slaughtered by the press and Howard.

I found the target again in a win over Notts County, but picked up an ankle injury in a challenge with Mark Draper. I rested and had painkilling injections, but it wasn't right. My final game of the season was at Tottenham Hotspur. We won 3-1, but soon after, I had an operation on my tendon, which put me out for the season. I got to the stage when I could not carry on.

I went to the remaining games and helped get the lads revved up. I was in the dressing room before the Sheffield United game, which proved crucial. What a match, unbelievable. The atmosphere was electric and the own goal by Brian Gayle to win us the game 3-2 was beyond belief. I went home and watched Manchester United play Liverpool. If Liverpool won, we were champions. At the final whistle, with Liverpool 2-0 ahead, it did not hit really me we were champions. Then the phone went. Champagne was popping. The celebrations against Norwich City a week later were fantastic.

Pre-season I carried on my rehabilitation, had four operations and did play a few games but I had no option but to retire. I loved my time at Leeds United. The squad was great and the craic was marvellous. Howard as a manager was brilliant, the best I played for. He was honest and looked after the players at difficult times. When Howard arrived at Leeds United, the crowds had slipped, but he turned it around and no team liked to play at Elland Road because it was an intimidating atmosphere for opponents.

Winning the Division Two and Division One championships capped off my career perfectly. I played for the team I supported as a kid, played for my country and won the top domestic honour with Leeds United, what more can a player ask? I see the Leeds lads from time to time and the banter is still there, which is magnificent. We often discuss the events of our 1989/90 campaign and especially that unforgettable day at Bournemouth. Winning promotion was the best feeling in the world.

CHRIS FAIRCLOUGH
CENTRE-HALF 1989–1995

BORN   12th April 1964, Nottingham
SIGNED   March 1989 from Tottenham Hotspur; £500,000 after initial loan
LEEDS CAREER   241 games, 23 goals
HONOURS   1 Division One Championship, 1 Division Two Championship,
7 England Under 21 caps
LEFT   Transferred to Bolton Wanderers, July 1995; £1 million

Chris was a stalwart defender during Leeds' two title-winning seasons
under Howard Wilkinson. An elegant footballer, Chris rarely made a
costly error. Quick, courageous, a firm tackler and tactically astute, Chris
won the club's Player of the Year award in his first full season. In 1991/92,
Chris scored two goals, including a crucial header against Coventry City
during the title run-in. Partnering Chris Whyte, the duo was a key factor
in the club's championship success especially when the pressure was at its
most intense.

Sheffield United 2 v Leeds United 3

League Division One
Sunday 26th April 1992

Bramall Lane
Attendance 32,000

The famous victory that ultimately clinches a third Division One title

Teams

Dave Bassett	Managers	Howard Wilkinson
Mel Rees	1	John Lukic
John Pemberton	2	Jon Newsome
David Barnes	3	Tony Dorigo
John Gannon	4	David Batty
(Sub. Dane Whitehouse)		
Brian Gayle	5	Chris Fairclough
Paul Beesley	6	Chris Whyte
Glyn Hodges	7	Gordon Strachan
		(Sub. Carl Shutt)
Paul Rogers	8	Rod Wallace
Alan Cork	9	Lee Chapman
(Sub. Ian Bryson)		
Brian Deane	10	Gary McAllister
		(Sub. Eric Cantona)
Carl Bradshaw	11	Gary Speed
Cork 28, Chapman (og) 67	Scorers	Wallace 44, Newsome 64
		Gayle (og) 77

Referee: G Courtney

I WAS ONE OF Howard Wilkinson's first signings at Leeds United. At the time, Leeds were in Division Two, but Howard had big plans to make them a force again. The coming seasons would bring title-winning campaigns, a Wembley appearance and European football. The great day out at Bournemouth was the highlight as a one-off game when we clinched the Division Two championship and promotion back to the First Division, but victory over Sheffield United two years later enabled me to win the biggest prize in domestic football. The match was also one of the craziest games I have played in.

Football was initially something I used to play in the street. Three of my four older brothers were keen footballers. Together with friends, we'd put jackets or bags down for posts and play all hours. Although I grew up in Nottingham and followed Forest's fortunes, like many youngsters I was not a staunch supporter, but followed the top sides of the era, who were Leeds United and Liverpool. Leeds had Bremner and Giles, while Liverpool had Keegan and Hughes, so kids looked up to them. I didn't have any real heroes, but I do remember watching the 1970 World Cup. Brazil stood out with the likes of Pelé, Gerson, Rivelino and Jairzinho. That era kicked off my passion for the game.

I represented my school, Nottingham City Boys, and went for county trials, but did not get into the team. It was competitive stuff. My break came when I was 13 and playing for a local club, Parkhead United. Scouts continually looked for talent on a Saturday and a Nottingham Forest scout spotted me. I attended various trials because at that time you could not sign until you were 14. This lasted until I signed schoolboy forms and I began playing for Forest Colts.

Brian Clough was manager, but we didn't train under him. Although we had signed for the club, there was no regular Saturday game; we only played occasionally. Most Saturdays I'd play for Parkhead United then the Colts group would come together for a game. When we reached the age of 16, Forest had to decide whom they would be signing as an apprentice. It was a nerve-wracking time, but fortunately, Forest offered me an apprentice contract.

Joining the club in 1980 was a fantastic time. Forest were European Cup holders, having retained the trophy with a win over Kevin Keegan's Hamburg, so it could not have been more exciting. I loved the club and was a big Forest fan on the back of the European Cup campaigns. I idolised all the players and still do. They had many star players including Peter Shilton, Martin O'Neill, John Robertson and Trevor Francis.

Brian gave me my first team debut against Tranmere Rovers. We won 2-0 and I enjoyed it immensely. I was nervous as hell beforehand, but Brian put me at ease. He said, "just go out there and enjoy yourself." There was no pressure on me. Forest had great coaches in Liam O'Kane and Ronnie Fenton, who were very protective of me as I was a young lad.

Now I am on the coaching side of the game, I see how Liam and Ronnie treated me. You pick things up from managers and coaches you work with. I never saw Brian Clough as a coach like you see now. He was a manager, who managed the team. Brian picked the team, motivated and inspired the team, but was not a tactical manager. His great strength was motivation, which is something I always try to work at.

Among many highlights during seven years at Forest, one game will always stand out, Celtic in the UEFA Cup at home in 1983. We drew 0-0 before claiming a brilliant 2-1 win at Parkhead. My abiding memory, however, was the atmosphere Celtic supporters created at the City Ground; it was fabulous. We reached the semi-finals, but went out to Anderlecht. It was a major scandal at the time following the referee's shocking display. Things happened in that game which had a determining factor on the result. We led 2-0 in the first leg before a 3-0 defeat. We felt gutted, but I still look back on the whole campaign with fondness.

I gained selection for the England U21s and captained the team on a number of occasions, which was a huge honour. Unfortunately, a full cap was not to be. Things were going along nicely when I broke an ankle at Luton Town towards the end of the 1984/85 season. After a double calf operation that summer, I came back pre-season, but pulled a groin and missed the whole of the 1985/86 campaign. It was incredibly frustrating and the worst part of my career.

After 18 months out, I came back against Arsenal. My contract was up at the end of the season, but I hoped to pick up where I left off. Unfortunately, contract negotiations were not good. In my heart of hearts, all I wanted to hear Brian say was, "I'm glad your back, here is a contract for a year or two years," but we fell out. I got frustrated and we both got stubborn. I just wanted to play first team football. It was time to move on.

First, I spoke to Howard Wilkinson at Sheffield Wednesday; I agreed to join, but then Tottenham Hotspur came in for me. I met David Pleat and decided to change my mind because Tottenham were a higher profile club. I was not happy to renege on Sheffield Wednesday, but I felt Tottenham would be a better move. It was a fresh start.

Pre-season I made sure I was really fit. Speed and fitness was the basis of my game. I really enjoyed my first year at White Hart Lane, but David Pleat was suddenly sacked and for three months, we waited for a replacement. Terry Venables eventually came from Barcelona. I played the whole season and looked forward to the 1988/89 campaign, but knew Terry would make changes. It was an uncertain time. I was in and out of the team with Gary Mabbutt and Terry Fenwick playing at the back. It was only a matter of time in my mind before I left.

Come transfer deadline, March 1989, Tottenham gave me permission to speak to Second Division Leeds United, which was fine by me. Howard Wilkinson was their new manager and rebuilding the club. I was a bit wary as I'd let him down before over the move to Wednesday, but the first thing Howard said was that whatever had happened in the past was water under the bridge. Howard wanted me to sign for Leeds United. Leeds was the only club that came in for me, whether there were others, I wasn't sure. One thing was for certain, Tottenham would not stand in my way as Leeds were in Division Two. Everyone in the game knew that Leeds had a great history and a terrific fan base, so with the right set-up there was every opportunity they'd bounce back to Division One.

Howard sold the club to me. He said that it was on the verge of something big. Howard knew what he wanted. He had a vision, but I still wasn't sure. Chairman Bill Fotherby then phoned me and he was convincing. Bill sold the club's ideas and Howard's ideas. He told me about the potential and determination that everyone had to get the club back to where they felt it should be. Howard wanted me to be part of the building process. Both made me feel wanted; a total contrast to Tottenham. I agreed to join on loan.

Gordon Strachan signed a few days before me. We made a winning debut against Portsmouth. Leeds were trying to reach the play-offs, but failed. I did not settle well or play to my potential, but was happy to make the move permanent. I was determined to have a good pre-season. I felt right, "let's really go for this." I was desperate to do it. I had a great pre-season, my hardest ever. It was what I needed. I could feel things coming together as new players like Mel Sterland and Vinnie Jones arrived.

Everything Howard said would happen was now materialising. We had characters and it bonded us. With the likes of Gordon, Vinnie, Mel and David Batty, there was plenty of Mickey-taking. We had a good group of lads, a genuine group of lads with no prima donnas and no rogues, despite what many said about Vinnie! We prepared in our own way. Gordon would not get overawed or overexcited. You just had to look at Gordon and you'd get a buzz. Plenty of comments about Vinnie were made, because of his hard man reputation. To me, Vinnie was just one of the boys, who gained his will-to-win and spirit at Wimbledon. Credit to Howard; maybe that was part of his plan. Wimbledon was famed for team spirit and togetherness. Vinnie could bring a touch of that to Leeds.

Initially, I partnered Peter Haddock, who was one of those quiet, but very reliable and efficient players. He did his job. Peter played centre-back and left back, got on with the job, but didn't get the plaudits like some names at the club. Gordon was captain and a real inspiration on and off the pitch. The team spirit that we had came from characters like Gordon. He was a big player, a great player and drove us forward. Gordon wanted us to get promotion. He did not want to come down a division from Manchester United and stay there. Gordon had the character, drive and talent. I was the same. We'd played all our football in the top flight and wanted to get back at the first attempt.

The team gelled together and led the way for most of the season. At times, we lacked a cutting edge and you cannot win championships unless you have a proven goalscorer. Howard recognised this and brought Lee Chapman from Nottingham Forest. Lee made his mark because he could make and score goals. The way we played with our full-backs getting forward, Lee was ideal to hold up the ball and allow our midfielders to join and score.

With one game remaining against Bournemouth it was between Sheffield United, Newcastle United and us. The title was still in our hands, but we had to win. Against Bournemouth, I had to mark Luther Blissett. My first thought was that I had to be on my game today. It was a hard, bumpy pitch and we had massive vocal support willing us to win the game. After 15 minutes, I knew we would win if we kept things tight and did not do anything stupid. The team had come so far; we were stronger and was not going to mess up on the last day. We claimed the win with a Lee Chapman header to clinch promotion and the title.

At the final whistle, supporters carried me off the pitch. I had my shirt, shorts and boots nicked. It was a brilliant atmosphere and a massive relief.

The highs of the game, the highs of being carried off, the applause and relief in the dressing room was brilliant. We'd set off to get up, a good group of players working for each other with a great team spirit. The supporters drove us on and off the pitch. We knew about the money that had been spent on new players. It had paid off. Team spirit and respect drove us on. It was our destiny to go up.

By the new campaign, Gary McAllister and John Lukic joined, further strengthening the side. We probably surprised a few teams by finishing fourth, but I don't think that you can 'overachieve' as a team. From a player's point of view, you go out to win every game. If you do that then you will win the league. That was my mindset. On the back of promotion, we knew the difficulties that lay ahead but we were in a winning mode. We had strengthened the squad; we wanted to win. I thought we were a good team and deserved what we got. We had an edge to our fitness and were organised. I had teamed up with Chris Whyte by now at the back and we complemented each other. Lee hit a rich vein of form and scored over 30 goals, which was phenomenal.

Before the 1991/92 campaign, Howard strengthened the team further by bringing in Tony Dorigo and Rod Wallace. Tony replaced Peter Haddock at left-back, who'd suffered a career-ending injury the previous season. Peter was not the only one to sustain an injury at left-back that season, there was also Jim Beglin and Glynn Snodin.

Howard wanted balance in the back four and now had it with John in goal, Tony at left-back, Mel at right-back and Chris and I in the centre. Part of our game plan was our defensive strength. It was something we worked on in training, was a means to an end, but that was how Howard wanted us to play. We played a high line, pushed up, let runners go if the ball didn't come and squeezed up. We did it well as a unit. John was not a vocal keeper, but was solid. He did his job well and kept the ball out of the net with spectacular saves at times. We needed Chris's height; I had the pace, so swept up behind him and the full-backs. Howard wanted Mel and Tony to get forward and it gave the team another dimension.

Our midfield was also solid with plenty of talent and plenty of goals. David Batty was more defensive, doing the box-to-box stuff. He retrieved the ball, which gave us a balanced midfield alongside Gordon, Gary McAllister and Gary Speed. In attack, Rod gave us energy and good pace. Teaming Rod with Lee Chapman, we had a strong line up especially with the likes of Steve Hodge, Carl Shutt and John McClelland to call upon.

We made a great start, but I picked up a knee injury against Southampton in our third game, which sidelined me for a couple of months. When I came back, the team was going well. It was easy to settle into a winning team. John McClelland had deputised for me, but I came back at Notts County. We won 4-2 and continued our good form. It was good to be back and good to be playing.

We played consistent football and exceptionally well in some games. I remember we thumped Aston Villa 4-1 when the game was live on television. It was terrific to get good reviews but I then got sent off in the next game against Everton. I did sometimes get a bit hotheaded. I saw the incident later on video and deserved to go because I raised my hands, but Rod came up trumps late on with a terrific winner.

We lost just one game before Christmas, which was some effort. It was becoming a two-horse race between Manchester United and ourselves. We'd played a couple more games than United and were a couple of points adrift, but we knew there was a long way to go with so many points to play for. It is a cliché, but as a player, you play one game at a time.

Just after New Year, we hammered Sheffield Wednesday 6-1. As with Aston Villa, the match was live on television. The Wednesday game sticks out in my memory not only due to our performance, but because I was captain along with Nigel Pearson who led Wednesday. Both of us had played for Parkhead United. I thought at the time, "that's not bad for two young hopefuls at that club." We won very well, so it was a great day.

Howard decided to strengthen further and brought Eric Cantona to the club. We were a bit surprised, as we did not know too much about Eric. As professionals, though, we were used to players coming in and moving on, so we just got on with it. The manager wanted him; Eric had no major impact on us. Eric was an attacker who could score goals, so was welcomed into our group.

We knew that we were in a challenging position with Manchester United still ahead, but you cannot look too far forward because you play games week after week. You come down from saying, "we can win it, we can win it," to thinking, "right, just one game at a time." Despite having played more games, we felt that our destiny was still in our hands. If we did not get over-excited or too nervous and just kept plugging away game after game then we knew that we could do it. We were going well, the media gave us a chance, but there was no way we were getting carried away with it.

Our attitude was spot on and it needed to be because with six games to go we got the right kick at the right time when we suffered a 4-0 drubbing at Manchester City. Most pundits wrote us off after that. We were now adrift by a point and had played two games more. The championship was over as far as they were concerned, but that was nonsense because there was still games left and anything could happen. OK, we were no longer favourites, but we were still in with a shout. There was still time to gather ourselves and have another surge. Albeit the result was devastating, but, timing wise, it was the best thing that could have happened to us.

Coming into the Easter fixtures, I was excited and nervous. The nerves did not hold me back, while the excitement drove me forward. The build up is nerve-wracking, but when you get on the field, nerves go. I felt, this is what it football was about. The daily grind of training each week was not my idea of what made being a pro enjoyable. We did a lot of 11 versus 11 across the width of the pitch. We played shape, style, possession and set pieces. It was not fun as in a traditional five-a-side or six-a-side type of game. It was methodical.

We beat Chelsea 3-0, when Eric scored a wonder-goal, and then got a hard-earned point at Anfield, which left three games. First up was Coventry City at home. Coventry was a solid team. Even though they had less to fight for, it would be tough. They hadn't been scoring many goals, but were also proving a difficult side to break down. The match was a late kick-off as it was live on television and we got a boost when news came through that my old club Nottingham Forest had won 2-1 at Old Trafford. It was a big surprise. We had a chance to edge ahead on points. It was a must-win game.

As expected, it was a tight game and we didn't make the breakthrough until the second half when I scored our opening goal. It was the most important goal I'd scored for Leeds. The ball popped up seven yards from goal. I didn't see Big Oggy, Steve Ogrizovich, come off his line, but did sense he was edging forward. I didn't have the cleanest of headers, but just managed to get my head on the ball. It was great to see the ball loop over Oggy into the goal. That put us 1-0 up. The atmosphere was electric; the tension in the air was great. We felt we would win this game. We got a penalty late on, which Gary McAllister put away for a 2-0 win. It was a game we had to win and did.

Back in the dressing room, we were delighted. The win guaranteed us a place in Europe, which was terrific. It was nine years since I'd last played in European competition, so it was something to look forward to, but our focus was on winning the league and making sure we'd be in the European Cup rather than the UEFA Cup.

Our win put massive pressure on Manchester United. We now had a one-point advantage. As important, United now had only one game in hand. They faced relegation bound West Ham in two days' time. Pundits predicted a Manchester United win, but we knew it would not be easy for them. West Ham were battling relegation and would not want to go down without a fight. That proved to be the case as the Hammers came good with a 1-0 win. The result meant that finally the destiny of the title was in our hands. I was not surprised because we'd always known it was a possibility. I think it shook a few of the newspapers up though, who had expected United to end their 25 year wait for a League title much more easily. But now it was down to us. Wins in our last two games, at Sheffield United and at home to Norwich City, would clinch the title, but we could not get complacent.

None of the lads acted as if the hard work was over. Our mental approach was, "we can do this, but we have not done it yet." All our energy and focus was on the next game. There were naturally nerves, but not ones that would knock you off track. They were the kind of nerves that inspired you to do what you needed to do, to achieve what we had worked so hard for all season. They were exciting nerves.

The match against Sheffield United took place at noon the following Sunday. Going down to the ground and seeing the crowd, the buzz was tremendous; the excitement was great. The build up you take in. Then it comes to the game; it's work and you are in a different zone. Howard named the same team that had defeated Coventry.

Sheffield came into the match in good form and fancied their chances, especially wanting to beat us because of the local rivalry and denying us the title, but we knew what was at stake. They had a solid defence and in Brian Deane had one of the league's most potent strikers. With a strong wind behind them Sheffield put us under a lot of pressure early on. The match was like a cup-tie, it was a real Yorkshire derby. Tackles flew in. In fairness, we made a slow start as Sheffield dominated possession. Glyn Hodges and Deane looked dangerous in possession, which meant that Chris Whyte and I had to be on our guard.

We experienced a few nerve-wracking moments, the worst when Chris cleared a John Pemberton strike off the line in the midst of a number of corner kicks. Sheffield were noted for their set pieces and often scored goals that way. That proved to be the case here as they took the lead just before the half hour mark. It was a bizarre goal that took a number of deflections, the last off Gordon, on the way to Alan Cork, who reacted quickest to score. It was a blow, but we had a resilient streak.

Tony Dorigo was wide with an effort at goal from a free-kick and as half-time approached; we began to get into the game as an attacking force. Gary Speed was looking sharp and, in Gordon, we had a player who could turn a game in an instant. Suddenly, we won a free-kick 40 yards out. Gordon took it quickly for Rod to chase. Rod got a touch as Sheffield keeper Mel Rees and centre-half Paul Beesley collided. The ball broke loose, Brian Gayle made a hash of his clearance, it hit Gary Speed on the shin before ricocheting off Rod past Pemberton on the goal-line. It was a madcap goal, but we didn't care. We'd equalised.

As we celebrated, Rees needed treatment and looked hampered when the second half began. With nobody to replace him, he had to battle on. Gordon's quick-thinking was his last input to the game as he was substituted at half-time due to a sciatica problem.

Carl Shutt replaced Gordon. Both sides probed for an opening. Rees was uncomfortable, but made a great save from Gary Speed in the opening moments of the second half, deflecting a goal-bound shot onto the bar. Gary went close again with two more strikes before John pulled off two great stops, one a terrific one-handed save to deny Brian Deane. The game was really in the balance.

Rees's unease, though, was obvious when we won a free-kick to the left of Sheffield's goal. Gary McAllister curled a terrific ball in, Rees got nowhere near the ball and big Jon Newsome stooped to head home. I jumped on him before Gary Speed joined in to celebrate. The image of us celebrating together appeared in newspapers the following day and is a permanent reminder of a magic moment. We had a 2-1 lead, but in this crazy game it would not last long.

Sheffield had a reputation for battling and quickly showed it from another corner when Pemberton, from a flick on by Gayle, shot across goal, and Lee Chapman could only deflect it into our goal. Just over 20 minutes remained with us locked at 2-2. A draw would leave the title back in United's hands. And it was anyone's guess what would happen next in this game, but nobody could predict the nature of what would turn out to be our winning goal and the goal which ultimately decided the destination of the title race.

Eric Cantona had replaced Gary McAllister and with his first touch headed the ball forward. It was not in a dangerous position for Sheffield, but their full back David Barnes looped the ball back towards Brian Gayle. Eric and Rod raced in to pressurise. Rees came out to clear. Gayle tried to nod it clear from just inside his penalty area, but put too much power on his header and could only watch in horror as the ball looped clear of Rees into the back of the net.

We could not believe it. The own goal put us in a great position, but it was not over, a single mistake and Sheffield would be back in it. Our bench kept us informed of how long remained and encouraged us non-stop. At the final whistle, we were delighted because we now had a four-point lead at the top. We just had to beat Norwich at home in our last game to win it.

The Sheffield match was bizarre. It was keenly contested and riddled with crazy goals. We played at times in a swirling wind, heavy rain and bright sunshine. It was not our slickest performance, but championships are not won on a day, it happens over a season.

Enormous pressure was now on Manchester United. If they defeated Liverpool at Anfield or drew then the title race would go to the last game. Any other result and the title was ours. But we knew there was plenty left in the season, it was not quite over. We knew the immense drive that Manchester United had, as they had not won the title since 1968. We knew they would not give up. They would fight all the way.

After the match, I wanted to go back to Leeds and share the moment with the lads. Some were going to Lee's place to watch United's game, but I had made plans to visit my parents in Nottingham after the game. I thought if I changed my mind, I might jinx the result. I went to Nottingham as planned and watched the United versus Liverpool match. It was surreal watching a game of football at my parents that at the end if Manchester United lost we were League Champions. At the final whistle, my dad and brother jumped up. I just sat still. Then dad grabbed my hand, shook it and said, "you've done it, son." That was really something because my dad was not the emotional type.

I knew it would be party time in Leeds, but I came up the following day. On the Saturday, we had the Norwich City game followed by a civic reception on the Sunday. It was a great atmosphere against Norwich, but I can't say that I enjoyed it because it was a game that we did not want to lose. As a defender, you had to stick to your guns. I approached it like any other match and we held out to win 1-0. Then the celebrations started. Looking at all the supporters celebrating after the Norwich game and at the civic reception, all I could think of was, "wow", a massive "wow".

Throughout the season, you know how much it means to supporters. You see it, you go out for a meal, a drink or to the shops and all people are talking about is the game. You know there is a massive buzz. Then when you see the celebrations, it brings it all into focus.

The highlight of my career as an occasion was getting promotion at Bournemouth. That will always be very special. That season there was a start, middle and an end. We started the journey pre-season, we played the games then had to win the last game to win the championship. It was fantastic. The title win in 1991/92 however, was a much, much bigger achievement. The feeling was different. It was my highest accomplishment in football.

Winning the Charity Shield at the start of the following season was a great occasion and turned out to be my only competitive game at Wembley. It was only really a friendly match, but it was a showpiece event and you do not want to go to Wembley and lose. You want to win. It was a great day out for supporters and players. It was a fantastic game, actually, with Eric Cantona scoring a hat-trick as we defeated FA Cup holders Liverpool 4-3.

Unfortunately, I was never fully fit during my last years at Leeds. I joined Bolton Wanderers where I experienced relegation and promotion again as Champions. It was satisfying, but not as satisfying as the first time with Leeds.

I still follow Leeds United's results. We had a good group of players and, although we don't see each other that often, as we have taken different paths, I look back on my time at the club with very fond memories. I enjoyed my football and played to my potential. Winning the First Division Championship was the biggest prize. The way we clinched it was amazing. Joining Leeds was the best move of my career.

DAVID WETHERALL
CENTRE-HALF 1991–1999

BORN 14th March 1971, Sheffield
SIGNED June 1991 from Sheffield Wednesday, combined fee of £275,000
along with Jon Newsome
LEEDS CAREER 250 games, 18 goals
HONOURS Coca-Cola League Cup runner-up
LEFT Transferred to Bradford City for £1.4m, July 1999

David had no first team experience when he joined Leeds United, but the
Chemistry student went on to lead Britain to a bronze medal at the World
Student Games and mature into a dependable and totally committed defender at Elland Road. Composed, quick, superb in the air and a strong tackler,
David became a stalwart in the Leeds defence alongside Lucas Radebe and
helped Leeds reach its first Wembley final in 23 years in 1996. Of his 18
goals, two came in impressive Premiership victories over Manchester United
during the 1990s.

Leeds United 1 v Manchester United 0

FA Premier League
Saturday 27th September 1997

Elland Road
Attendance 39,952

Leeds United overcome the defending champions with a battling display.

Teams

George Graham	**Managers**	Alex Ferguson
Nigel Martyn		Peter Schmeichel
Gunnar Halle		Gary Neville
		(Sub. Phil Neville)
David Robertson		Denis Irwin
Lucas Radebe		Gary Pallister
David Wetherall		Henning Berg
David Hopkin		David Beckham
Alfe-Inge Haaland		Roy Keane
(Sub. Robert Molenaar)		
Gary Kelly		Paul Scholes
		(Sub. Ronny Johnsen)
Bruno Ribeiro		Karel Poborsky
		(Sub. Ben Thornley)
Rod Wallace		Teddy Sheringham
Harry Kewell		Ole Gunnar Solskjaer
Wetherall 34	**Scorers**	

Referee: M Bodenham

DURING MY CAREER at Leeds United, there was no bigger game than playing Manchester United. They were the dominant team of the decade, so to get one over them meant a lot, to not only the players, but also our supporters. There was, of course, a history between the clubs. We had not beaten Manchester United at home since 1980, or in any game since 1981, so everyone celebrated our 2-1 win in September 1994 like we'd won a Championship. I scored that day and three years later, hit the target again to give us a 1-0 win. It was my most memorable goal for Leeds.

I was born on the Sheffield Wednesday side of town. My dad was a Wednesday-ite, so I grew up supporting them. Wednesday were in Division Two, so many of my heroes such as Brian Hornsby, Mel Sterland, Mark Smith, Peter Shirtliff and Tommy Tynan were not household names at the time. Jack Charlton was manager. The game that sticks out was an FA Cup semi-final defeat to Brighton in 1983. I was devastated. Everything that could go wrong did. Our coach broke down on the way to the game. We got to the ground as the match kicked off. It was a strange day. I'd loved to have gone to a cup final, but it was not to be. Then Howard Wilkinson took over and we gained promotion to Division One. They were great days.

I'd played for my school, Sunday league football since I was 10 and represented the city team when suddenly, a Wednesday scout spotted me. Being a Wednesday fan, I didn't think twice about signing for them, but never got started because I had a growth disorder. Some bones were growing at different rates, so I missed 15 months. For a kid of 13, it was a pain to put it mildly sitting out sports, but Sheffield Wednesday stayed patient.

When I started training again, letters were sent out about players being retained. I got one saying that I wasn't. My dad rang up and asked why because the club had not seen me play. The club said there had been an administrative error. I had another chance and things snowballed for me. Wednesday wanted me to sign apprentice forms, which was fantastic, but I also wanted to continue my A-levels at school. Wednesday agreed.

When it came to the end of my A-levels, I asked if I could combine a football career with studying chemistry at Sheffield University. Howard

Wilkinson had been to university, so was understanding. At the time, I took this for granted, but as I got on in football, I realised how lucky I was. Over the next two seasons, I had been an unused first team substitute once for Wednesday when an opportunity came to join Leeds United, who Howard was now managing.

Wednesday's youth team coach Mick Hennigan had become Howard's assistant at Leeds. When things got going at the club, Mick recommended taking a chance on Jon Newsome, who had played a few games for Wednesday, and me. Mick knew us inside out and had monitored us as we went on to become regulars in Wednesday's reserve team that won Pontin's League Division One in 1990/91.

I had a year to go on my degree course, so it was a stipulation of mine that I would complete the course and not throw away the previous two years. Howard agreed. People have often asked me whether I regretted my decision as I could have had three more years' playing full time. I have no regrets. There was no guarantee I'd make it and I had the academic ability to complete my degree. I could have broken my leg on the first day at Leeds. Many players go out of the game at an early age; I wanted to make sure that if that happened to me I had something to fall back on. I've never known how the £275,000 fee was split, but Jon was probably £274,500 of that because of his experience!

We arrived at Leeds at the start of the 1991/92 season that would end in Championship glory. While completing my degree I represented the British Universities at the Student Games, where we won a bronze medal. Playing in the Games was fantastic, but it was galling because the previous games were held in China. For our tournament I travelled five miles down the road as the Games took place in Sheffield. It could have been more glamorous!

Most people think you do a few hours of lectures each week at university, but doing chemistry I went in every day, so it was a case of getting up to Leeds when I could. During the season, I played in the reserves. A number of players helped me early on, especially 'Robocop', John McClelland. To have someone of John's experience alongside me in the reserves guiding me through a game was tremendous. John was a big influence. I did play two minutes of the championship-winning campaign against Arsenal. I was due to come on when we were 2-1 down, but then Lee Chapman scored. I thought that my chance had gone, but I did come on after 90 minutes and played centre-forward against Tony Adams and Steve Bould. That was a baptism of fire.

With my degree over, pre-season 1992/93 I began full time training. Howard was very involved in training sessions every day. He was a hands-on manager and open to new ideas. At Wednesday, pre-season meant endurance-based running, but at Leeds, we did more power-based work. People thought Howard was stubborn – once his mind was made up that was it – but he took on the latest thinking in terms of the scientific side of football.

I was on the bench for the Charity Shield. Going down to Wembley was a fantastic experience. I was incredibly nervous about maybe getting on. It was a marvellous occasion and gave me a feel for things. It made me more determined to be part of the first team squad.

The atmosphere was great after winning the title the year before, which brought tremendous team spirit. I used to travel from Sheffield to Leeds every day with Carl Shutt and Dylan Kerr. Gordon Strachan was at the centre of most Mickey-taking and Carl was the butt of most jokes in the dressing room. I had to listen to his moaning all the way home about the stick. It was great. As a young lad coming into the club, I had no trouble settling in and got on very well with the likes of Gordon, Gary McAllister and Gary Speed from the start.

Although I'd made my first team debut, I never counted that really as my debut as I was only part-time. We got off to a poor start in 1992/93 and, with the first team struggling, I got an opportunity. I travelled down to Southampton with the squad. The night before the game there were a few rumours that my initials, DW, was on the set pieces sheet. Howard, however, did not tell me that I would be playing until lunchtime of the game when we had our team meeting.

I was extremely nervous, but I was looking forward to making my first full appearance. Before the game, John Lukic came over to give me some great words of wisdom. I got on really well with John. He said, "listen, if things start going wrong all you have to do is panic." I thought, "thanks, John!" The game went well for me and we drew 1-1. I was marking Kerry Dixon, the former Chelsea striker, for most of the game, but late on went down with cramp. Maybe the nervous excitement and warm weather got to me. On the flight back, a few of the journalists said, "well done." It was a good day. Making my first team debut was memorable. It was a great feeling to know that I could play at this level. It did not matter how confident I was in my own ability, you had to prove it and I felt that I had taken a step towards doing it that night.

I played in two cup-ties against Scunthorpe United, but was left out of league games for a while apart from a heavy defeat at Manchester City. Just before New Year, I got a recall for my full league home debut against Norwich City. I was more nervous for this game than the Southampton match, especially as I was marking Chris Sutton, who could be a real handful. Again, the match went well for me and we kept a clean sheet in a 0-0 draw. I was delighted.

Towards the end of the campaign, I made a few more appearances, which was a big step. To get games in my first full season was very pleasing. It was also satisfying to get my first goal for Leeds in a 1-1 draw against Chelsea, a glancing header. Training day in and day out was tough, but I knew that I would go from strength to strength.

The club had endured a disappointing time after winning the title, finishing seventeenth, and wanted to get back to where they were, so it was difficult to see a young, inexperienced centre-back becoming a regular. All I could do was keep the confidence in my own ability, work hard in training and take chances when they came. David O'Leary joined during the close season and immediately went into the first team, but suffered an injury after a few games and I was back in to the team.

Playing alongside Chirs Fairclough helped develop my game. I tended to attack the first ball, while Chris swept up behind. It was a period of transition as the likes of David Batty, Lee Chapman, Mel Sterland and Chris Whyte moved to other clubs or retired. Carlton Palmer and Brian Deane came in. Teams change, it happens at every club. It is part of the game. Our target was to get 40 points then kick on. For me it was important to play more games and that progressively built up. I wanted to be an important part of the team week in and week out.

We enjoyed a far better campaign, finishing fifth. I played over 30 games that season and scored a memorable goal in a 2-0 win against Liverpool. I had no problem with our supporters. I was learning. People maybe thought that at 22, I may not get much better, but I knew that I would learn and was willing to learn. My best years at Leeds were still to come and my relationship with supporters reflected that.

In 1994/95, we again finished fifth. One result stood out and that was a 2-1 win against Manchester United at Elland Road. Leeds supporters always look forward to a clash with the Red Devils. The rivalry is intense and the build up to this game was massive. Leeds had edged them to the title in 1991/92, but Alex Ferguson's team had bounced back and were now defending Premiership champions, having won the double in 1993/94. United had quality players throughout the team with the likes of

Schmeichel, Bruce, Pallister, Ince, Hughes and Giggs. The win meant so much to Leeds fans.

To cap a great day, I scored. People said Manchester United didn't play well. In my view, we didn't let them play well. Early on, we got a corner; a couple of their players missed the cross at the near post. The ball hit Steve Bruce in the middle of the chest and sat up in front of me right in front of the Kop. I tell everyone that I gave Schmeichel the eye, looked in one corner and put it in the other, but I totally miss hit my left foot shot into the corner. It was a great moment and the goal still makes me smile. The noise from the Kop when I scored was incredible.

Brian Deane had struggled for goals in his first season and had not scored this time around. There was a lot of pressure on him and it weighed on him, so to score our second goal was great for Brian. It gave him confidence. We battled for everything and chased every ball. We knew this could be our day and the relief at the end, knowing that a ghost had been laid to rest, was tremendous. It was a fantastic feeling.

Tony Yeboah arrived at Elland Road during the season, I had not heard too much about him. I still remember his first training session on the old training ground where the car park is now and he could not hit a barn door from five paces. Everybody looked at each other thinking, "what have we got here?" But Tony quickly proved his worth. Tony's power, pace and finishing was amazing. For me, Tony is up there with Jimmy Floyd Hasselbaink, who would join us in 1997. Jimmy was a lethal finisher, but Tony was more spectacular and his goals helped get us into Europe. We ended the season superbly and I could not wait for the new campaign.

At the start of the 1995/96 season, Tony's goal against Liverpool was unbelievable and just as unbelievable was his strike at Wimbledon. I had a great view of the Liverpool goal especially. It is one, which will live long in my memory as it rebounded down viciously from the bar and ricocheted back up into the roof of the net like a bullet. The campaign was a season of highs and lows. We started well in the league and went well in both domestic cup competitions, but it fell apart. The European adventure summed it up.

We played Monaco in the first round and did not know what to expect. We arrived at our hotel when it was dark. It overlooked the whole bay, I thought, "I can't wait to see that in the morning." When I saw the view, I thought, I want more of this European adventure. Then to the game and some of Monaco's players had great reputations. For most of our team, it was a new experience, so to win 3-0 was amazing. Tony got a sensational hat-trick and we defended well. For the second leg, it put us in a strange position. With our limited European experience, we seemed unsure whether to attack or defend and, it turned into a nervous occasion. Monaco won 1-0 and had other chances to turn the tie around, but we hung on.

We faced PSV Eindhoven in the next round. The first leg at Elland Road we lost purely down to inexperience. PSV scored early on and we felt that we had to win the tie in the first half. It ended up attack against defence, there was no midfield stalemate; it was all out attack from both teams. To lose 5-3 was very disappointing after getting back into the game at 3-3. In the return, they were too good for us.

We reached Wembley in the Coca-Cola Cup; everyone was really looking forward to it. For me, it was my first final, but ended up as a massive disappointment. We had injury problems, players played out of position and we came up against a very good Aston Villa team, which is often forgotten. Our big players did not perform and it was a real struggle. It was such a bittersweet day. As it is the only major cup final I'll play in, you have to take something from it. I'll never forget the build up. A few days earlier, we'd gone out of the FA Cup. The results affected the rest our season as we slipped down the table.

There was always going to be a lot of pressure on Howard because of the fans' reaction at the cup final and his reign ended when we lost 4-0 at home to Manchester United a few games into the 1996/97 campaign. Losing by four at home was not acceptable, especially against your arch rivals. There were always going to be repercussions. It was a sad end for Howard, but he had made his mark at the club in terms of success.

George Graham took over. His first comment was that we would do well to stay up, which was a bit puzzling, but we finished the season safe, scoring the least ever number of goals. We had five centre-halves in the side as we were playing Lucas Radebe and Mark Jackson in midfield. George set his stall out to stay up and we did it. As a defender, working with George was great as we worked on the defensive side of the game. Every player knew his job.

In contrast George's first full season in charge was terrific. Nigel Martyn, Lucas Radebe, Gary Kelly, Lee Bowyer and Rod Wallace were at the club and George brought in David Hopkin, Alfe-Inge Haaland and Bruno Ribeiro. George had also purchased Jimmy-Floyd Hasselbaink and youngsters like Harry Kewell were about to make their mark, but we made an indifferent start, especially at home. We had gained a creditable draw with Arsenal, but had gone down to defeats against Crystal Palace, Liverpool and Leicester City. Our away form, though, was solid as we had won a remarkable match at Blackburn 4-3 and defeated Southampton 2-0.

Our home form needed to improve and we now faced Manchester United, again League Champions. The match would prove to be the highlight of my Leeds United career. Manchester United had a team of household names and was the dominant team of the era. They had won four Premiership titles in five years and were favourites to go all the way again. They didn't have the dream midfield of Keane, Beckham, Scholes, and Giggs playing on this occasion, but still had a great side out, while we had a stronger squad than in recent years.

Nigel Martyn was the best keeper I played with. He was a great shot stopper, confident and controlled the box. I have a lot of time for Gunnar Halle and Gary Kelly. Gunnar was underrated, a great professional and always dependable. Gunnar got up and down the pitch; he was a manager's dream. Gary has not done badly for a right-winger playing out of position! It's good to see him back and playing so well because some people said his best ways were over. Lucas Radebe really progressed under George. In the first training session, we did some one against one work and Lucas came into his own. There was a change in Lucas and he got better and better. He was a fantastic player to play alongside in central defence.

Alfe was a running machine. He had amazing stamina. For me as a defender Alfe was great because he covered so much ground and broke up attacks, I liked playing with him. Bruno looked like he would be around for a long time, but things never quite worked out for him, which was a shame as he had a smashing left foot. David Hopkin was more creative and wanted to get forward. David had spells at Leeds when he looked as if he would be a fantastic player, but again he did not fulfil that potential.

Rod Wallace was a great lad and probably was a bit underrated. Rod had fantastic ability and looked like he may make the international side, but it was not to be. He scored some incredible goals, none better than a brilliant solo effort against Tottenham Hotspur in 1994 that won a 'Goal of the Season' award. Rod had terrific pace and on his day was difficult to handle.

Harry Kewell was only a teenager back then, but was a real talent. Harry had power, pace and possessed so much technical ability. In his early days at Leeds, Harry was exceptional.

As for Jimmy Floyd Hasselbaink, Jimmy was never short on confidence. We got on really well. At first, Jimmy ruffled a few feathers when he arrived from Boavista, because Jimmy being Jimmy came into the club as if he owned it. Jimmy wanted to know why he would have to run a yard to collect a pass instead of it going to his feet, and he let everyone know. We soon let Jimmy know what the score was and he settled. Jimmy was a great signing. He was strong, powerful, hard to dispossess and had a terrific strike. I struggle to separate Jimmy and Tony Yeboah as being the best striker that I played with.

When I first came to Leeds United, I was not aware of the massive rivalry between Leeds and Manchester United or the size of occasion when the clubs lock horns. I was also not aware that it had been 14 years since Leeds had last claimed a home victory against Manchester United, so the match had escalated into an enormous event. To be a part of that 2-1 win in 1994, which ended that dreadful run, was fantastic and, over the coming years, I always looked forward to our clashes. We had another great win on Christmas Eve in 1995. Tony Yeboah scored a cracker and Brain Deane grabbed a goal in a 3-1 win. Leeds supporters enjoyed the festivities that year.

The build up during the week was always hectic. The media interest was immense, the local newspaper usually produced a special edition looking ahead to the match and tickets were virtually impossible to get. As you got to the ground on match day there were so many fans milling around, it was incredible. We always got a good reception, but for Manchester United games there were far more fans around early on.

Before kick-off you could sense it was not a run of the mill game. For Manchester United, the atmosphere was different to normal. You sat in the dressing room preparing and could hear boos as the United team bus arrived. You knew it was a special day for supporters and then the atmosphere when you came out on the pitch is amazing.

A year on from our 4-0 defeat against United at Elland Road, only four players from that game were in the starting line up. We knew it would be a tough game and that was how it turned out. I remember the lads encouraging each other before kick-off. Although United were a strong team, there was a feeling among the lads that maybe we could surprise them again.

The first half was a cagey affair with few clear-cut chances. Gary Kelly was covering a lot of ground on the right side of midfield and went close with a header, while Bruno Ribeiro and David Hopkin worked tirelessly. Without Jimmy leading the line, Rod Wallace used his pace to unsettle United's defence. In terms of possession, the match was pretty even and Nigel Martyn had one shot of note to save, which came from a David Beckham effort.

Just after the half hour mark came my magic moment, the best moment of my Leeds career, as we took the lead from a free-kick on the left. As usual, I jogged forward to support the attack. Gary Kelly swung a ball into an area where Gary Pallister, who was marking me, thought Schmeichel was going to come. All I was interested in was the ball. I saw it coming across and I was determined to get my head on it. Schmeichel hesitated, which gave me a yard to nip in front and I managed to plant the ball in the corner.

It was a great moment for me and I did lose it for a couple of minutes. Things were a bit of a blur. I scored some important goals during my career and you can lose it in the heat of the moment. When you get back to your position, it takes time to calm down and that is when you are at your most vulnerable. The more experienced you get then you deal with moments like that better, but it took a bit of time that day! I was fortunate enough to score against United before, so to do it again in front of the Kop was special.

At half time, we were satisfied, George told us to keep it tight. He felt sure that Manchester United would raise their game and the pace of the match. That would give us a chance to catch them on the break.

As we anticipated, United dominated the second half for long periods. We got our tactics spot on, though, George sent us out to play virtually as an away side to counteract United's counter-attacking style, which was always dangerous. We worked hard in midfield to close down Keane and Scholes and restricted the supply line to Solskjaer and Sheringham.

United rarely threatened our goal. They did create a few good openings, but in Nigel we had a keeper on top of his game. He had already produced a fine stop to deny Beckham, but reserved his best to deny Sheringham with a flying save before palming away a close range header from Pallister.

Fifteen minutes from time, the complexion of the game changed when United, having used all three substitutes, lost Keane through injury after he made a terrible challenge on Alfe. That tackle would have huge repercussions for both their careers. United's 10 men were now up against it and changed tactics by throwing caution to the wind, which played right into our hands. At every opportunity, they started to launch the ball forward, which you did not expect a Manchester United team, but they got a bit desperate.

Everything landed on my head. It was one of those days where the ball was a bit of a magnet. We still had to be wary, though, because the referee added on six minutes of injury time, which seemed to go on forever. It always seems that way against the big clubs. We almost grabbed a second when Rod Wallace fired just wide and had one late scare, but Solskjaer blazed wide.

In the end, one goal was enough – and it was mine. We had battled away and got our reward for a fantastic win. It was a great performance. As a personal highlight, it is definitely my best memory playing for Leeds United. Scoring the only goal and keeping a clean sheet edges it over the game against Manchester United we won 2-1 that I also scored in, but both are particularly memorable games.

I hadn't scored for 16 months, then suddenly I'd scored two in three games. The result kick-started our season, we thumped Newcastle United 4-1 in our next home game and enjoyed some amazing results, none more than against Derby County at Elland Road when we came from 3-0 down after 20 minutes to win 4-3. When you're 3-0 behind, you think at the time, "help!" but it was a game when we hadn't played badly, but football can do that to you sometimes.

Every chance Derby had, they scored. You think, "what happens if we do play badly?" but we got the bit between our teeth and began to claw our way back. In the second half, we got back to 3-3 then I had a rush of blood and found myself in the penalty area! Lee Bowyer put it straight on my head six yards out with just the keeper to beat, but I managed to put it wide. I thought, "we won't get a better chance," but then Lee popped up with the winner. It was an untypical George Graham performance, but was a tremendous game to play in.

We hammered Derby later in the season 5-0 on the back of a 4-0 win at home to Blackburn, completing another double. We finished the campaign in fifth place, once again qualifying for Europe. I thought, "hopefully we'll fare even better next time around," but I did not get a chance to find out. Early on in the 1998/99 season, David O'Leary took over from George. It would prove to be my last season at Leeds. I was disappointed to leave.

At Bradford City, my goal against Liverpool in the final game of the 1999/2000 season kept my new club in the Premiership and helped Leeds, who I still had a great affinity for, get into the Champions League. It made it a memorable day to say the least. If I could have written a script, I could not have written a better one. Alongside the goals I scored for Leeds against Manchester United for different reasons, that goal was a highlight in my career.

When I look back at my time at Leeds United, I have an overriding sense of great affection. I arrived from Sheffield Wednesday and Leeds was a real rival, but eight years down the line, Leeds United was my club. I arrived as a part-time player and left with 250 appearances to my name, played in Europe and in a cup final at Wembley. The fans have always been and are still to this day fantastic to me. Leeds United will always be a special club to me. I always enjoy going back to Elland Road. I have some fantastic memories of my time at the club, and none more than the day I scored the winning goal against Manchester United, which brought terrific celebrations for supporters.

DOMINIC MATTEO
CENTRE-HALF 2000–2004

BORN   28th April 1974, Dumfries
SIGNED   August 2000 from Liverpool, £4.25 million
LEEDS CAREER   146 games, 4 goals
HONOURS   6 Scotland caps
LEFT   Free transfer to Blackburn Rovers, July 2004

Dominic played in midfield and defence during a four-year spell at Leeds United. A product of the Liverpool School of Excellence, Dominic, was a hit with supporters. Dedicated, tactically astute and possessing a never-say-die attitude, Dominic was a key member of the team that reached the Champions League semi-finals in 2001 and entered club folklore following his goal against AC Milan in the San Siro Stadium. Appointed skipper for the 2002/2003 season, despite missing numerous games through injury, Dominic played a pivotal role as Leeds escaped relegation. The crucial result came in an unforgettable win at title-chasing Arsenal.

Arsenal 2 v Leeds United 3

FA Premier League
Sunday 4th May 2003

Highbury
Attendance 38,127

Leeds United avoid relegation with an astonishing victory against the title-challenging Gunners

Teams

Arsène Wenger	**Managers**	Peter Reid
David Seaman		Paul Robinson
Kolo Toure		Danny Mills
(Sub. Nwankwo Kanu)		
Ashley Cole		Ian Harte
Oleg Luzhny		Lucas Radebe
Martin Keown		Michael Duberry
Ray Parlour		Gary Kelly
Gilberto Silva		Dominic Matteo
Sylvain Wiltord		Eirik Bakke
(Sub. Jermaine Pennant)		
Robert Pires		Harry Kewell
(Sub. Giovanni Van Bronckhorst)		(Sub. Simon Johnson)
Thierry Henry		Mark Viduka
Dennis Bergkamp		Jason Wilcox
Henry 30, Bergkamp 62	**Scorers**	Kewell 5, Harte 48, Viduka 88

Referee: K Barratt

I PLAYED IN MANY high profile games for Leeds United in the Premiership and Europe. Most supporters I know would expect me to select as my most memorable match the night I scored in the San Siro in the Champions League and yes, it was a marvellous occasion. For me, though, there is one game I will never forget because so much depended on it.

It came at the end of the 2002/03 season when we faced a trip to Arsenal, who had to win to stay in the race for the title. One more match remained for us at home to Aston Villa, but we knew a win at Highbury would guarantee our safety. It was a very different atmosphere to the glory nights in Europe as we prepared. Nobody gave us a chance and we could not have been playing tougher opponents – Henry, Bergkamp, Pires for starters – but we dug deep to claim a fantastic win. The celebrations afterwards were unforgettable, the relief enormous. As captain, I was delighted for the players and loyal supporters at the match, who had followed us through a turbulent campaign.

I was born in Dumfries, but raised in Southport. Liverpool scouts spotted me at the age of 10, when I was playing for a local junior team called Birkdale United. I attended regular training sessions at the Liverpool School of Excellence, which was fantastic for a young kid. I played in different positions to begin with, before settling at centre-back.

My parents couldn't always take me to the academy due to work commitments, so other players' parents helped with lifts. Without their support, I'd never have made it. I signed schoolboy forms at 14 and joined as a YTS player at 16. As an apprentice, we did various jobs before being bussed to the Mellwood training ground. At the end of the apprenticeship, I signed a full contract with Liverpool. Having the chance to develop at the academy was great.

Steve Heighway, who starred for Liverpool as a player, is the club's Academy Director, and played a major part in my development. Steve had a hard side, but his advice and coaching helped. From the start, Steve encouraged me. You only need to look at the number of lads that have come through the academy to play at the highest level to see how successful Steve has been. Before me was Steve McManaman, then Robbie Fowler and, of course, Michael Owen, Steven Gerrard and Jamie Carragher have since made it.

It's hard to say why some lads make it and others don't. Like many, I had ability, but I did the simple things well. That is how I've always played. For me it was about giving everything in that red shirt. Whichever team I have represented, I've never changed that philosophy.

When I was a trainee, Ian Rush, Ray Houghton, Mark Wright, Bruce Grobbelaar and John Barnes were among the star players. Then there was Ronnie Whelan, Barry Venison and Steve Nicol, who I used to get a lift in every day off. They were all good lads. As a youngster coming through, I learned so much from John Barnes. When you watched John train and play, it was impossible not to pick up things. He was a great professional. I was just breaking into the team when John was Liverpool captain. John was great with the young lads. I made sure, when I was a captain, that I was always on hand for the young lads at the club.

It was an amazing time and, of course, being a Liverpool supporter, to actually meet and play alongside some of your heroes meant everything to me. I made my debut in midfield against Manchester City in 1993, then got selected at left-back. Being a utility player helped me get into the first team regularly because there were four experienced central defenders ahead of me, but it was tough holding down a first team spot.

I was involved in a couple of cup final squads, which was a tremendous experience at such a young age. I remember going to the Worthington Cup final at Wembley when Steve McManaman scored two goals against Bolton in 1995, then in the FA Cup final when Manchester United won with a goal by Eric Cantona a year later. I was gutted not to play against United. You never know, I might have changed the game.

I was in and out of the first team, but finally seemed to make a break-through during the 1999/2000 campaign. I signed a five-year deal, but then heard Liverpool was signing a player in a similar position to me. I was told I'd not have a guaranteed first team place. I'd be on the bench again. I knew in my own mind that it was time to move on.

When Leeds United made an inquiry for me, I knew that my days at Liverpool were over. I needed a new challenge. I didn't know at the time, though, that I was injured. I'd played pre-season for Liverpool, taken part in the last game at Anfield, and got through without any problems. At a medical, doctors found a problem with my right knee on a scan, but it wasn't causing any discomfort and a deal was agreed.

Leeds had a thriving academy. Harry Kewell, Alan Smith, Gary Kelly and Ian Harte had come through the system. Paul Robinson and Jonathan Woodgate would soon join that list. They also had experience in players like Nigel Martyn, Lucas Radebe, David Batty, Danny Mills and Lee Bowyer. I joined just after Mark Viduka and Olivier Dacourt. It was a great squad.

Manager David O'Leary had high hopes we would be challenging in the Premiership and would go well in the Champions League for the first time. Leeds had edged Liverpool out of third spot on the final day of the previous season, when they drew at West Ham, while Liverpool lost at Bradford City. As the season developed, Rio Ferdinand and Robbie Keane joined to boost our challenge.

In the Champions League qualifiers, Alan Smith scored a crucial goal against 1860 Munich to get us into the group stages. We were all looking forward to playing at the big stadiums and facing the best players. As a foot-baller, you want to play against the best teams. In the Premiership, playing against Liverpool, Chelsea, Arsenal or Manchester United you know that you'll have to raise your game. It was the same in the Champions League. Every game is so difficult you have to be switched on. If you don't then you'll get punished.

Certain games stick out from the first group stage. My Leeds debut came in our Champions League clash at home to AC Milan. It was a big game for not only me, but also my family as my dad is Italian. I played left wing that night. It was lashing down at Elland Road. Last minute, Lee Bowyer hit a speculative shot; and Dida dropped it into the back of the net. We won 1-0. It was a great start. Besiktas away was a tough game, but we got a draw and then hammered them at Elland Road. I scored one of my rare goals that night. Of course, I also scored in the San Siro against AC Milan. We drew 1-1. It was a massive night. Back in the hotel, Eirik and I had a few bottles of red.

There were so many memories as we progressed. Against Real Madrid at home, with Zidane pulling the strings, we got a right lesson, but we probably deserved to beat them away. Anderlecht away was probably my best performance. They were a very hard team to beat at home, but we crushed them 4-1. Lazio was a great performance and then there was Deportivo La Coruna in the quarter--finals at home. It was an amazing game and the atmosphere was incredible. Every game was so different. Our home form was so important. Any team coming to Elland Road, with the exception of Real Madrid, got a tough game.

Going through the tournament, I didn't really think about winning the Champions League as there were so many hard games coming up. You could not get too far ahead of yourself, but when we defeated Deportivo, especially after the away leg when we got such a lesson, you thought, "right who have we got in the semis?" It turned out to be Valencia. They were a very good side, so I thought, "don't get beat in the home leg, get an away goal in Valencia and we have a chance." We got a 0-0 draw, but it was not to be, nevertheless what a campaign.

At every game, there were so many Leeds fans. I knew lots of lads that travelled to the games, especially away. It was fantastic for them and the atmosphere they created was amazing. A highlight of course was the singsong in Rome and Milan on the pitch after great results against Lazio and Milan. An incredible bond developed between the supporters and players. Leeds fans still sing a song about my goal against AC Milan, "Dom Matteo, He's our captain-o, Scored at the San Siro, Dom Matteo", which is terrific.

When I first played for Liverpool, having stood on the Kop, there was a special bond. Playing for Leeds in those games brought it all back to when I first started playing football. When you grow up in Liverpool, then play for them, it is special. It's been a number of years since I left, but whenever I go back there are still faces that I recognise. You don't forget them and they never forget you. I always get looked after well by Liverpool folk.

That season we had a great result in the league at Anfield, winning 2-1. We played really well that day and needed a win to stay in contention for a Champions League place. Our victory came in the middle of a purple patch of results. We'd made an indifferent start to the Premiership campaign, but had some fantastic results early on, none better than when we defeated Liverpool at Elland Road 4-3, Mark Viduka got all our goals. After New Year, we really kicked on, but ultimately just missed out. It was a massive blow, but still we would be playing in the UEFA Cup, which was some consolation. After playing in the Champions League, though, that is where you want to be competing.

We had a great spirit at Leeds United and a very strong dressing room. There was a long list of Mickey-takers that included David Batty, Jason Wilcox, Jonathan Woodgate, Alan Smith, Michael Duberry and even myself. We were all involved and it all helps build rapport. At one stage, quite a few of us were living in a hotel. We were young, so you tend to mess about. Some days we went over the top with certain things, it was a great time.

It had been a great season and to cap it I made my international debut for Scotland. I had already represented the England U21 side a few months after joining Leeds. Now I was selected to play for Scotland against Australia. It was my first full international cap. I was eligible to play and it was a massive honour. Unfortunately, after winning six caps for Scotland, I was forced to retire from the international scene due to recurring injury problems.

People have often asked me if I regretted leaving Liverpool, because they won three cups that season. Of course, you think what might have been if I had stayed. I had a five-year contract, the likes of Gerrard, Carragher and Owen came through and they claimed more honours, but there was no guarantee I'd have been part of those teams. Plenty of players have come and gone since me. I moved on and have no regrets.

In 2001/02, Leeds endured a difficult season. It started so well and it was great to be playing alongside Robbie Fowler again when he joined, but the New Year saw our form dip and we missed out on playing in the Champions League again, which was a massive disappointment. Towards the end of the season, David O'Leary hinted to me that he was going to make me skipper when Rio was out for a game at Aston Villa. I was shocked, but delighted.

During the summer, there were many rumours and eventually Terry Venables replaced David O'Leary as manager. I got on fine with David. He picked me every time that I was available. Other players may have a different opinion, but David was good for me. He gave me my chance at Leeds United. David was straightforward, he said if you worked hard in training then you had every chance of getting in the team and was as good as his word. For me David was a good manager. As a player, you get used to managerial changes. It is part of the game. Just as new players come in and out of a clubs, so do managers. Whatever your personal feelings you just get on with playing.

Before a ball was kicked in 2002/03 Rio joined Manchester United for £30 million, so there was going to be a new captain. I think Eddie Gray had some influence, as he knew all the lads, but it was great to take over. To captain a club like Leeds United was a huge honour. As a kid, I dreamt of becoming a captain of a big club. I wasn't able to achieve it at Liverpool, so to do it at Leeds on a permanent basis was terrific. Away from leading the team out on a match day, I had to represent the club at functions and presented quite a few awards at schools and clubs. It was great because it gave me an opportunity to give something back to the community.

On the field, I knew I'd give everything, but there are 11 players on a pitch, so it's about everyone pulling together. I knew the players well and didn't think we were that far away from winning a major trophy, which is what we all desperately wanted, but it was not to be and turned into a really tough season.

The frustrating thing about that campaign was that we started brightly, defeating Manchester City and West Brom comfortably in our opening two games, then picking up great wins over Newcastle United and Manchester United. From mid-September though, it was downhill. By the festive games in December, we'd slunk back down the table and knew we were in for a hard slog. We were also out of the Worthington and UEFA Cups.

I was injured for a long period and it was hard watching on from the sidelines and not being able to help the lads. Between the win over Manchester United and an FA Cup third round win at Scunthorpe, I played just three games. I enjoyed a brief run of eight games when we completed our only double of the season against West Ham, but missed our exit from the FA Cup in the quarter-finals at Sheffield United, which was a bitter disappointment. All that remained was one target – avoiding relegation.

Major issues concerning the finances of the club were happening off the field, but the players can only influence things on it. It was up to us to climb away from the relegation zone. A new chairman, Professor Jon McKenzie, had replaced Peter Ridsdale. Peter Reid was appointed caretaker-manager following the departure of Terry Venables. Of the squad, Jonathan Woodgate, Robbie Keane, Lee Bowyer and Robbie Fowler had departed, which frustrated supporters and understandably so, but the players remaining were good enough to get us away from relegation. Peter Reid added a spark and some much needed belief.

I came back into the side for a trip to Charlton Athletic with seven games remaining. It was Peter's second game in charge and we were fighting for survival. We hammered Charlton 6-1. It was a great performance and gave us confidence. Mark Viduka was back on song and kept a recent run of goals going with a hat-trick. Harry Kewell grabbed two goals. Mark scored two more in a draw against Tottenham Hotspur before we went down to defeat at Southampton. We bounced back with a win over Fulham before another defeat at Blackburn Rovers. Two games now remained; an away trip to Arsenal and a home game against Aston Villa.

I felt far more pressure playing in a relegation match than challenging at the top of the table. The difference is immense. Playing at the top, it isn't easy, but it's a lot easier than playing at the bottom where you are scrapping for survival. Every game is like a cup final as you build up to it. It is so important to try and get something out of a game. Every time you lose, the pressure to win the next one builds up and it continues like that week after week. The pressure and tension is never-ending.

When you are winning, everything seems to go for you in a game. You get the breaks. Many games you may not play well, but you come through and win irrespective. But when you are down at the bottom everything seems to go against you. It's weird. You go out and think that everything is going to go against you; it gets into your head. Away from the game, it gets into your life. You're unhappy, it affects your family life. It was not an easy time, but all you can do is keep playing and battling away, hoping results and your luck may change.

The night before the match against Arsenal, which was live on Sky Sports, the lads in the hotel really felt the pressure because on the Saturday, fellow strugglers West Ham had picked up a surprising win against Chelsea, while Bolton had drawn with Southampton. We were now equal on points with both clubs, but did have a better goal difference. A draw was not that good for us, as we'd still need something from our last match. A win would guarantee us survival, but Arsenal had to win to stay in the title race.

I shared a room with Eirik Bakke and when we went to our room we were chatting about the game. I could not sleep at all. Next morning, we got up and I remember looking at the Arsenal team sheet with Reidy [Peter Reid]. Peter joked, "this lot are shite. We'll hammer these today." They only have Henry, Pires, Bergkamp, Seaman, Cole and Keown, and on the bench, there is Kanu and van Bronkhorst. Peter's comment broke the tension.

We set our stall out to make life difficult for Arsenal. We knew they would attack us from the start, so played with Mark Viduka operating as a lone striker. Paul Robinson was in goal. Lucas Radebe came in for Alan Smith, out through suspension, and slotted into the centre of defence alongside Michael Duberry and full-backs Danny Mills and Ian Harte. I moved into midfield with Gary Kelly, Eirik Bakke and Jason Wilcox. Harry played wide on the left flank.

Arsenal were without Sol Campbell and Patrick Viera, which was a bonus for us, but they still had a formidable side out. Very early on, we had an escape from a Pires corner when Gilberto hit the bar, but we stunned the crowd by opening the scoring after a few minutes. And what a goal it was. Jason Wilcox began the move with a long ball to Harry Kewell wide on the left. Cutting in at pace, Luzhny and Keown could not get close to him and without breaking stride, Harry struck a brilliant curler left-footed past Seaman from 25 yards.

It was the perfect start and we had clearly rattled Arsenal because a few minutes later, Harry almost scored again after being put clear by Mark Viduka. Harry rounded Seaman, but the angle proved too difficult to cut the ball back into the net. It was close, though. Without Campbell, Arsenal seemed unsure in the centre of defence. Mark had a couple of half-chances and should have done better from a pinpoint cross from Ian Harte.

Arsenal seemed surprised, but came back strongly. Paul Robinson made a great save from a deflected shot by Henry then tipped a strike by Parlour onto the bar. We'd had an escape, but soon found ourselves pegged back when Henry found a yard of space to head home an equaliser. We had to withstand a whirlwind Arsenal assault then. Michael Duberry came to the rescue to hack clear off the line from another long range effort by Parlour and we were thankful just before half-time to an alert linesman when he flagged Wiltord offside when he forced the ball over the line after Henry had hit a post.

It had been a tough half and we had withstood a lot of pressure, but we had also created chances. Half-time had come at just the right time for us as Arsenal had started to create real problems for us, but the break disrupted their rhythm. We came out for the second half fired up and again caught Arsenal cold inside a few minutes. Our chance came from a free-kick awarded against Cole 20 yards out. Ian Harte stepped up and, as he had done on so many occasions before, fired home a great effort. An absolute rocket. Seaman had no chance.

We could not have asked for a better opening to the half, but, as expected, Arsenal came at us with everything and after pinning us back, equalised again when Henry and Pires linked to set up Bergkamp for a simple finish. 2-2. Upping their tempo with the win they needed to stay in the title race with Manchester United, we were really up against it. Bergkamp was just wide with an effort and then Henry hit a post again. Maybe, this was our lucky day.

Arsenal's desperation showed in some frantic play at times. We sensed an opportunity. Harry went close with an effort, which Seaman only just saved, before being substituted.

The minutes ticked by and a draw seemed a good result, at least leaving our destiny in our own hands, but that meant we had to win our last game to ensure we survived. We just wanted one last chance. Suddenly it came two minutes from time, when I managed to dispossess Arsenal substitute Pennant wide on the right. My long ball found Mark Viduka in space. Arsenal defenders claimed offside, but Mark killed the ball, dragged it back, wrong-footing Luzhny, before steadying himself brilliantly and steering the ball left-footed beyond Seaman into the corner of the net. Another fantastic goal.

We'd done it. The celebrations after were wild. It was an incredible win. On the day, nobody gave us a chance, but we went out, played really well and scored some great goals – and because of that it's a match I'll never forget. The lads battled unbelievably well on the day. It meant so much to us all. We knew the stakes at Highbury. Everyone gave that little bit more. We pulled together and put in a fantastic performance to pull off a result every big as bit in Milan in terms of its importance, and arguably against a better team, who were in full flow, challenging for the title. I remember seeing the Leeds fans after the game. You could see in their faces what our win meant to them.

It was a difficult season, but in many ways as a team, we did not do ourselves justice. Our home form was the problem; we won six games compared to seven away from home. Against Arsenal, we showed that we could compete with the best. At the time, it was so important. I thought, "well, we got through the season." It had not been a good year, but we stayed up. We came away relieved and hoped we could move forward – of course it's well documented that hope was not to be.

In 2003/04, we suffered relegation. Behind the scenes issues did affect players to a certain degree. Players were at different stages of their careers, so had different opinions about what was going on, but I would not hold that as the reason why we got relegated. As a team, we were not good enough. None of the lads had experienced relegation before and it is by far the worst feeling I have experienced in football. The dressing room after our defeat at Bolton was a terrible place to be, we all felt so numb. I was also gutted for our supporters, who did not stop singing even when it was clear we would be relegated. They deserved better. I did not want to leave Leeds, but everyone is aware of the financial situation at the time. The club has done well to recover to the extent that it has.

When I look back over the four years that I was at Leeds, I played with many great players. Nigel Martyn was a superb goalkeeper and fantastic to play in front of; it gave you so much confidence having him behind us. Nigel was a good talker, commanded the penalty area and made unbelievable saves. Paul Robinson learned an awful from Nigel, training with him every day and working with him. Paul was just coming through, but you could see that he was going to get to the top. Robbo was a tremendous shot stopper and a real talent. And of course now he is firmly established as England's first choice goalkeeper.

Gary Kelly has been a fantastic servant to Leeds and was great to play alongside because he was so steady and experienced. Ian Harte was another great guy, not only because he gave us balance on the left, but also as he scored so many important goals and they were never tap ins. Ian was really dangerous from free-kicks and scored all kinds of goals whether blasting them in or bending them into the top corner. Ian added another dimension to the team.

Lucas Radebe was a player that we all admired. Lucas was a role model in the way he played the game. He always had a big smile, you can speak to any player we faced, they always had one of their toughest games of the season when playing against Lucas. He was a top player. Rio was a class act and a great player to play with. Rio's reading of a game and anticipation were superb and he was so comfortable bringing the ball out. We worked well as a pairing in central defence. When Rio left, Jonathan Woodgate came in and played a similar game. Jonathan was very comfortable on the ball and loved playing for the club.

In midfield, we had many talented players. David Batty was a major reason why we won lots of our games. Batts sat in front of the back four, didn't let anyone through and was a great team player. Olly Dacourt was also a big part of that team and then there was Lee Bowyer. Both were good footballers and had different skills. Olly was so strong, while Lee was non-stop up and down the pitch. He also joined the attack to score many important goals.

Harry Kewell was one of those players who had so much ability. When he was one-on-one against an opponent, he could do anything. Harry could skin you, or take it on the outside or inside. For a defender, he was tough to mark. Harry could also strike a ball venomously and scored some fantastic goals. Harry was a great player.

Then there was Smithy. I was very close to Alan Smith and we spent a lot of time together. We were both single, so shared many experiences together as we both matured as players. Alan played his heart out every game for Leeds. The day Leeds went down, I felt the lowest of the low then

I looked at Alan and just gave him a big hug. You only had to look at him and could see how much it was hurting.

As for Mark Viduka, he was a great player to play with. Mark's strength and skill on the ball was fantastic. Robbie Keane was brilliant every time he played for Leeds. I would have loved to see him play more games and obviously, it was great to play again with Robbie Fowler, he was such a natural finisher whose career at the club was blighted by injuries.

Looking back over my career, I have been very fortunate so far. At Leeds United, I competed at the highest level, captained the club and experienced unbelievable ups and downs. I had a very special relationship with Leeds supporters, which is something that means a lot to me. Whenever I go back, I always get a great reception and at away games, they still sing about my goal in the San Siro, which is amazing. The Leeds fans deserve better and I hope that it is not too long before they are back in top-flight football because that is where they deserve to be. Leeds United supporters are incredibly loyal, without a doubt the best.

I have so many fantastic memories from my time at Leeds, but none better than the feelings of relief and elation after defeating Arsenal to avoid relegation to stay in the Premiership. It was a great game, but there were many nerve-racking moments. When Arsenal equalised twice, the lads showed tremendous character to go on and win. Before the game Reidy told us to go out and enjoy it. We did.

PAUL BUTLER
CENTRE-HALF 2004–PRESENT

BORN   2nd November 1972, Manchester
SIGNED   July 2004 from Wolves, Free transfer
LEEDS CAREER   94 games, 4 goals (up to and including 31 August 2006)
HONOURS   1 Republic of Ireland cap

Paul has been a key player in the heart of Leeds United's defence since arriving in 2004. It has not been an easy task leading the team at a period in its history when it has had to move forward after virtual financial meltdown, but with Paul as skipper, a new side has emerged with the task of winning promotion back to the Premiership. Resolute, a strong tackler and a leader by example, Paul helped Leeds reach the Championship play-off final in 2006, before losing out at the Millennium Stadium to Watford. As a new era dawned, there were encouraging performances and none more so than an amazing comeback at Southampton, which epitomised the club's never-say-die spirit. Paul scored Leeds' opening goal on the way to a remarkable 4-3 win.

Southampton 3 v Leeds United 4

Championship
Saturday 19th November 2005

St Mary's Stadium
Attendance 30,173

Leeds United make arguably the most dramatic comeback in the club's history after trailing by three goals with 19 minutes remaining

Teams

	Managers	
Harry Redknapp		Kevin Blackwell
Antti Niemi		Neil Sullivan
Rory Delap		Gary Kelly
Michael Svensson		Dan Harding
Claus Lundekvam		Paul Butler
(Sub. Tomasz Hajto)		
Danny Higginbotham		Matthew Kilgallon
Marian Pahars		Frazer Richardson
(Sub. Neil McCann)		(Sub. David Healy)
Nigel Quashie		Shaun Derry
Dennis Wise		Liam Miller
(Sub. Ricardo Fuller)		
Matty Oakley		Eddie Lewis
Theo Walcott		Robbie Blake
Brett Ormerod		Rob Hulse

	Scorers	
Pahars 27, Quashie 35, pen 45		Butler 71, Blake 77, Healy 84 pen, Miller 86

Referee: I Williamson

SINCE MY ARRIVAL at Leeds United back in July 2004, so much has happened at the club. Players have come and gone, but throughout we have battled away to take the club forward. Missing promotion last season was heartbreaking for everyone connected with the club, particularly, we know, our loyal supporters – but the lads are determined to bounce back. When an overview of last season is put together our win at Southampton will certainly feature at the forefront and it is a game that supporters will talk about for years to come.

As a player, when you look back at your career, there are certain games that you keep a video of, along with a match programme and shirt you wore. Our victory at St. Mary's last season was one of those games and is already a highlight of my career. I scored our opening goal in a quite incredible fight-back. It kick-started our season and we almost went all the way in the play-offs. Our victory was one for the record books, so to be involved was fantastic. The spirit displayed by the lads as we clawed our way back into the match is something that I will never forget along with our incredible supporters, who surpassed themselves that day.

I grew up in Manchester and played football at Mostyn Brook School, which is where the head of History, who just happened to be a Bradford City scout, spotted me. My teachers were firm; they said if I did not do my schoolwork, then I could not play for the school team. A few lads at Mostyn Brook made it in the professional game including Remi Moses, who played for Manchester United. I played Sunday League football regularly in Manchester, which is when I heard both United and City were interested in looking at me, but it was too late as I'd already signed associate schoolboy forms at Bradford and everything kicked on from there.

As a kid, I was a Blue, so Manchester City was my team and I could not wait to see them play at Maine Road. My Uncle John took me to watch City and I used to sit on the Kippax wall for years. Growing up, being a defender, I followed the fortunes of Tommy Caton and Paul Power at Manchester City. As I got older and got to know the game a bit more as a player, I admired players like Arsenal defenders Tony Adams and Steve Bould, who I had the pleasure of playing with at Sunderland.

I started my football career first at Bradford City, where the manager was Terry Dolan, who was a great influence on me; but he left to join Rochdale. After around a year Bradford let me go, which I was not too disappointed about because I had been homesick. I went home and soon joined Terry at Rochdale, which was a great move for me because I played against the likes of Billy Whitehurst, a legendary, physical brute of a lower league centre-forward. You always learn as a youngster playing against the likes of him.

At Rochdale, I really grew up and after six years moved to Bury, where, in my first season, 1996/97, we won the Second Division championship, which was a massive achievement. Getting into the First Division, the Championship as it is now, was amazing for a club the size of Bury and staying up was an even bigger achievement, but we battled away and deserved it. It's a bit like Wigan staying up in the Premiership in 2005/06, which was a great accomplishment because no pundits gave them a chance.

After a couple of years, Sunderland came in for me and in my first season, 1998/99, we romped to the Division One title by 18 points, which was incredible. I was now able to test myself in the Premiership. It was tough marking the likes of Thierry Henry and Andy Cole, but I really enjoyed the challenge. Unfortunately, I got injured during pre-season 2000/01. Peter Reid was manager at the time.

I wanted to play first team football but it took me until November to get back from injury. I went out on loan to Wolves and enjoyed my time at Molineux. I asked to join Wolves on a permanent basis, but Peter said no at first. Two months down the line, we were still arguing about it. I was not happy, so pestered Peter every day and eventually he agreed to let me join Wolves in January 2001. I was relieved as I could move forward again with my career.

I enjoyed my time at Wolves. We won promotion to the Premiership in the play-offs in 2003 with a memorable 3-0 win over Sheffield United. It was an unbelievable experience. Sheffield had enjoyed a great season. They were favourites in the final as they had reached two cup semi-finals during the season, but we came out on top and deservedly so. Kevin Blackwell was the Blades' assistant manager and reminded me of our win when I came to Leeds United two years ago.

Joining Leeds United was a new and exciting challenge. I could have stayed at Wolves, they offered me a new contract, but I felt that I'd done my time at Molineux. I'd achieved what I set out to do, which was to help get them into the Premiership. It was down to the club to spend in order to have a chance of staying there, but they didn't really do that, which is what you have to do. Everywhere I have played, I have achieved something, so I am holding out for success here at Leeds.

No disrespect to Wolves and its own history, but Leeds United is one of the biggest clubs you can play for. They have a rich history and I wanted to become part of it. I spoke to Kevin, who'd just been appointed manager, and he said that it was a new era for the club at the start 2004/05. He was going to clear the decks and wanted me to lead it from the front. I have not regretted my decision to come to Elland Road one bit.

When I came to Leeds, Kevin asked me to be club captain and I jumped at the opportunity. I enjoy the responsibility. I spoke to Gary Kelly and other senior players; they backed me fully, so that was great to know. It was a massive challenge, though, because so much had happened at the club since their relegation from the Premiership in 2004 with all the comings and goings of players. It was important to get the squad to bond quickly, so we could get a good start.

When it comes to captaincy, to some extent you try and model yourself on people who have been great leaders in the game. Players such as Bryan Robson at Manchester United and Tony Adams of Arsenal. They are players that you cannot help but be inspired by. As a player over the years, you learn from various captains that you have played with at clubs. At Sunderland, I deputised for Kevin Ball, who was a terrific servant, and there was Steve Bould who had vast experience. Then at Wolves, there was Paul Ince, who I shared the responsibility with and Dennis Irwin, who had won everything at Manchester United.

You take features from individuals that suit your own personality and character, but in the end, you have to go out, play your own game and be your own man. If there is a need to get a message across from the touchline, I'm on the field to deliver it, but we also have a number of experienced players who know the game, so we are continually communicating, which is great. I have always been vocal on the pitch, I may not always get it right, but there is always a meaning to what I say, and the lads know that I am only saying certain things for the benefit of the team.

It's an honour to captain any club and especially one with the tradition of Leeds United. Down the years, the club has had great captains. You only have to look around the stadium and see the pictures of former skippers like Billy Bremner, Gordon Strachan and Lucas Radebe on the walls, but that comes with the territory here at Elland Road.

Kevin told me that he was going to give me the captains' armband because of my experience at Sunderland and Wolves getting the lads together. At Wolves, they signed a lot of players in my first year at the club. It was similar to Leeds at the time. Kevin said there would be many players coming and a lot of players going. He needed to know that the dressing room spirit was right. It's been brilliant. I have been in a lot of good dressing rooms, but in terms of spirit and togetherness this has been the best dressing room I've been in.

There are always jokers at every club and we have had our share here. Some of the former players like Michael Duberry and Seth Johnson were real characters. Now, Gary Kelly, Shaun Gregan, Robbie Blake, all the old guard really, are crucial as they have been in so many dressing rooms; they know how to encourage the young kids to take up the mantle. It has been a testing time from the start. When I came in two seasons ago, Kevin said he had certain players lined up to sign, but two weeks into pre-season in Denmark and Norway, it appeared those players would not be coming. Kevin apologised and said that the money was gone; transfer fees coming in were paying bills. It was a shock because I'd dropped down to a team that was favourites like Wolves to get back up straight away as they could attract players. It was a case of battling away and we did.

At first, there were times when we really did not know which way the club was going to go, then Mr Bates took over and we have not looked back. Last season was a massive achievement for the club because as players and a group of staff, we set a target to get into at least the play-offs when the outlook from fans was probably a top-10 finish, which would have been an improvement on the year before.

To jump into the play-offs and, in fact, nearly get automatic promotion was a massive achievement. The play-off final was a one-off and you have to accept what happened on the day, but we must build on that. We have got rid of the negativity around the club. I don't like using the term 'laughing stock' because Leeds United was labelled as that for a while. That label I believe has now gone and we must continue to build. We will be among the favourites for the league this season, which shows just how far the club have come in two years.

We made an inconsistent start to last season, but stayed in contention and thoroughly deserved our play-off place. We played the form team, Preston, in the semi-final. They had come off a great run in the final few games. It appeared the toughest tie and it proved to be, but we drew the home leg 1-1. We showed great character coming back from a goal down. It was a full house. Alan Sutton, our physio, has been at the club years and he said afterwards that the atmosphere took him back. The noise inside the ground that night was unbelievable. I was out injured, but I'd never heard anything like it. I'd love to hear it regularly every home game.

When we travelled down to Preston for the return leg, to many pundits, they were favourites. I was injured again, so stood on the sidelines and the lads put on probably the performance of the season in the circumstances. To withstand the hostility we had in a tight little ground, we only had 2,000 of our fans when we could have sold 25,000 it was that big a game, and come out with a win under that much pressure was fantastic.

Leeds United's travelling supporters are second to none, the places they fill is just unbelievable. In recent years, we have not had any tangible success, yet we are still filling the stadiums away from home and that shows the draw of the club. At Plymouth in my first season, we won 1-0. It was a midweek game and was the first time the stadium had sold out all season. There were over 20,000 inside and it was a cracking atmosphere.

When Wolves went down that season as Leeds, they could not attract as big a crowd to Plymouth. All the big names were at Wolves, but the Plymouth fans came out to see Leeds United play. It does not matter who wears the Leeds strip, fans want to see the white shirt with the Leeds badge on. There is a lot of pressure on players to carry this mantle because of what has happened in the past. You have to have a strong character or you get found out quickly.

Leeds United fans are very knowledgeable and they can quickly work out if you have the guts or not to play for their club. You either sink or swim. You may not be the most talented player, but if you show heart and commitment, supporters will appreciate that. With the number of players that have come in, that is something I have noticed. If you try on the pitch and don't leave anything in the dressing room, the fans will be there for you.

Last season, we made a reasonable start and stayed in contention for a play-off place throughout the season. When you look back, of course, there was the disappointment at the end, but you must also see how far we have come from when I first arrived. The turning point in many ways came at Southampton. It was an amazing match.

Our comeback was simply incredible. I played in a match for Wolves when we came back from 3-0 down to win 4-3. The big difference then was that we scored five minutes into the second half to get some momentum and then every 10 minutes afterwards. Gary Kelly had been part of a Leeds side that overturned a three-goal deficit against Derby County, but again they had reduced the score before half-time. Neither of us had ever known a team come back from a three-goal deficit with just 19 minutes left and doing so after performing so poorly in the first half. It was quite unbelievable.

In that first half we gave away three soft goals and were heading for a defeat, which on the balance of play was clearly deserved. Striker Marian Pahars, who was back in the Saints' side after a long layoff, returned to score with a close range header and midfielder Nigel Quashie, who dominated midfield, grabbed Saints' other two goals, one a penalty on the stroke of half-time when Dan Harding handled an Oakley cross. Southampton's Theo Walcott, who was receiving plenty of praise in the media for his obvious talent in the press at that time before being snapped up by Arsenal, was also giving Matthew Kilgallon a torrid time.

There was little that we seemed to be able to do right and we could have been four or five goals behind at half-time to be honest. Its hard to say why we played so poorly, nothing clicked for us at all and we were severely punished. As we walked off the field, Southampton players were high-fiving each other. They clearly felt the game was won and it was hard for anyone to disagree with their viewpoint based on the way we had performed; or more to the point had not performed.

In the dressing room during the interval, nobody said a word at first. We just sat there stunned. Kevin came in and talked about passion. We knew that we'd let ourselves down and our supporters down. The gaffer said, "I've got nothing to say. Just get out there and play with some pride for those fans stood behind the goal."

We went out and I felt if we got beat 3-1 or 3-2, at least we'd have won the second half, but nothing happened for the first 25 minutes. In fact, we were thankful to Neil Sullivan for two outstanding saves to keep the score as it was. There seemed no way back.

Halfway through the second half, Kevin brought David Healy on for Fraser Richardson, which gave us some fresh legs, but I was looking at the clock and thinking, "we're running out of time." Suddenly, we won a corner. As usual, I jogged forward to join the attack. Gary Kelly's cross came over, I met it with my head and its 3-1! I thought, "well, at least we've got a consolation goal." Then in the next 15 minutes, I've never played in a game like it in my life. All hell broke loose. Suddenly, we were breaking forward, winning tackles and with our fans driving us on, the impossible became possible.

David Healy was causing trouble every time he was in possession, Liam Miller was becoming an influence, and six minutes after my goal, David set up Robbie Blake, who had run non-stop. We were back in it at 3-2. Our supporters were now going hysterical. We had 4,000 fans at St. Mary's Stadium and incredibly, although we faced an impossible-looking task at half-time, they were out-singing the Southampton fans, chanting, "We're gonna win 4-3." In my 15 years as a professional footballer, I'd never seen support like it that Saturday afternoon. They did not really expect us to come back, but they were determined to make their presence felt.

Thirteen minutes were now left and anything was possible. It was game on. The odds were still against us, but a shift in the match had taken place. We were now in the ascendancy and Southampton, who had looked so assured, now seemed edgy. Their confidence had gone and six minutes from time, Higginbotham handled a shot by David Healy for a penalty. David had only been on for a few minutes, but was so cool to make the score 3-3. Our supporters went crazy, mobbing David. I could see Southampton had gone. They were just holding on and we sensed it. Lining up, I looked at Gary Kelly. He was screaming, "come on, we can win this!"

Two minutes later, from another attack, Rob Hulse got himself into a great position, he had a chance to shoot, but spotted Liam Miller in a better position, pulled the ball back and Liam crashed home what proved to be the winning goal past a distraught Antti Niemi. The comeback was complete. There was no way back for Southampton. At the final whistle all the players and staff got into a huddle, it was a fantastic moment and one to savour.

Back in the dressing room, just as we had sat down dejected at half-time and hadn't said anything, well, again we sat down and didn't know what to say, only this time because we could not believe that we'd come back from 3-0 down. It was difficult to take in at first. It was an incredible fight-back.

All our goals had come in a 15-minute period and we could have had another one or two at the end as they desperately pushed forward trying to get an equaliser. We had won, though, and our feat did slowly sink in. It was a huge win and we realised that if we could go to Southampton and win then we could go anywhere and win. Without any doubt, it was a massive turning point in the season for us and we kicked on. We may have ultimately missed out on promotion in the end, but we took a significant step forward that day and our aim has to be to go one better.

It was some triumph. What people often forget is that Southampton had been on a great run when we played them twice in a short space of time. We led them in the table by two points, but Southampton had lost only two games, one at Elland Road, which we had nicked 2-1. They were something of a draw specialist, having drawn 10 out of 17 games, but we knew they would be very difficult to beat, especially at home, where they had conceded just two goals.

At the time, they had a big squad; no disrespect to teams after Christmas that went down and got results, but we beat them when only Peter Crouch and Kevin Phillips had left. We beat them when they had the Quashies, the Pahars and the Walcotts. It was much more of an achievement because they had all the big hitters playing. They were still a Premiership side in many ways and were clear favourites before the game because of that squad.

Our victory will always stay in my memory and has already entered Leeds United club folklore. I was delighted for the players and also for our fans, who had been incredible throughout. That win illustrated our team spirit and our loyal supporters deservedly revelled in it. It was an unbelievable experience and fans still come to me with a programme from that day as a souvenir for me to sign because they know that is has gone down as an all-time great game for Leeds United.

I've seen the play-offs from both sides now and it is a massive occasion in terms of the build up. The calls you get and the amount of tickets that you have to order for people is incredible. It's the biggest final in the world, as its worth £30 million all told, which is more than the Champions League final. It's a lot to carry as a player, but that is what you are in the game for, matches like these. You're 90 minutes away from getting your club back to where you believe it belongs and I'd love to be associated with that achievement.

At home, if Leeds can get a winning team on the pitch, then I believe the fans will return. I played here for Wolves and Sunderland when there was a full house and there is no more intimidating ground as Preston found out when they were over 30,000 Leeds fans urging us on. That is what we need now. We've got ourselves established over the past two years, we have been through the rough times and have developed a squad that will be competitive.

Neil Sullivan has been there and done it. He is respected in the game; he's an international and a fantastic keeper. I take my hat off to him because he's moved out of London in his 30s as he wanted a challenge. He has been unbelievable since he's been at Elland Road. Sully is experienced and gives us confidence. Some of the saves he's pulled off have been incredible. Sully is a terrific shot stopper and commands the area. They say a good old 'un is better than a good young 'un. That is not always the case, but Neil breeds confidence on the pitch because he's got that name on his back; Sullivan.

The same can be said about Gary Kelly, his name speaks for itself. Gary's been here years and rightly his picture is on the walls. Gary has been a great servant to the club. I've gone on record as saying there will not be many more testimonials at Leeds United. We had the Chief, Lucas Radebe, last year, but in the modern game, it's very rare for someone to achieve 10 years at a club. Players in the future will not be as loyal as Gary. He had offers to go elsewhere, but stayed.

Sean Gregan is very similar to me. He's a winner and has tremendous experience. He is another 'captain' that we have here and he's great to play alongside. The bigger the occasion then the more Sean comes to the fore. Then there is young Matthew Killgallon. He has it all, but he needs another couple of seasons where he is comfortable. Matthew has pace to burn and I have no doubts that he will step up a level. Steven Crainey has suffered with injuries, so we have not seen the best of him, but I expect a lot from him.

In midfield, Steve Stone has tremendous experience. He suffered a bad injury that took all of the 2005/06 season for him to get him fit. We missed Steve big time. Steve's experience will be vital for the club to move forward. Then we have the workhorse in midfield, Shaun Derry, who gets through so much work. Shaun played through injuries and was a crucial member of the team. As for Eddie Lewis on the left wing, he is an international with bags of experience and a sweet left foot.

Rob Hulse did a great job up front, but has now moved on to Sheffield United. Robbie Blake has always scored goals at this level. He's a real box of tricks, gets the ball at his feet and will score. Then there is David Healy _ Sir David after he scored against England for Northern Ireland to win that World Cup qualifier. He's another one that scores regularly at this level. Richard Cresswell has been a big loss with his injury for a period, but once we get him fit, we'll have a potent strike force also with young Jason Beckford, who is learning his trade and Ian Moore.

Saying we want promotion back to the Premiership is all well and good, but the lads can see that we came so close. We have been there and the lads know we can get there again. The next step is getting into the top two. It's a big call for us, but for a number of us in our 30s there are not many years left to get into that top flight.

At Leeds United, I have not achieved anything yet, but there is no reason why we can't. We proved that on our day we can defeat anyone from the most difficult of circumstances. If you can come back from 3-0 down at Southampton then you can come back from anywhere. If we show the same spirit and togetherness as at Southampton, Leeds United will soon be back in the big time.